AUGUSTINE ON ROMANS

Society of Biblical Literature

TEXTS AND TRANSLATIONS
EARLY CHRISTIAN LITERATURE SERIES

Robert L. Wilken and William R. Schoedel, Editors

Texts and Translations 23
Early Christian Literature Series 6

AUGUSTINE ON ROMANS
Propositions from the Epistle to the Romans
Unfinished Commentary on the Epistle to the Romans

by

Paula Fredriksen Landes

AUGUSTINE ON ROMANS
Propositions from the Epistle to the Romans
Unfinished Commentary
on the Epistle to the Romans

Paula Fredriksen Landes

Scholars Press
Chico, California

AUGUSTINE ON ROMANS

Propositions from the Epistle to the Romans
Unfinished Commentary on the Epistle to the Romans

Paula Fredriksen Landes

© 1982
Society of Biblical Literature

Library of Congress Cataloging in Publication Data

Augustine, Saint, Bishop of Hippo.
   Augustine on Romans.

   (Early Christian literature series ; 6) (Texts and translations, ISSN 0145-3203 ; 23)
   English and Latin.
   Bibliography: p.
   Includes indexes.
   1. Bible. N.T. Romans—Commentaries.
I. Landes, Paula Fredriksen. II. Augustine, Saint, Bishop of Hippo. Epistolae ad Romanos inchoata expositio. 1982. III. Title. IV. Series. V. Series: Texts and translations ; no. 23.
BR65.A793E5   1982   227'.107   82-10259
ISBN 0-89130-583-1

Printed in the United States of America

alla mia nonna

Expositio quarundam propositionum ex Epistola ad Romanos, reproduced from the 10th-century manuscript written at Cluny, now Paris, B.N., Latin Nouv. acqu., 1449, fol. 64r.

Table of Contents

Introduction	ix
Abbreviations	xv
Expositio quarundam Propositionum ex Epistola ad Romanos	2
Propositions from the Epistles to the Romans	3
Epistolae ad Romanos Inchoata Expositio	52
Unfinished commentary on the Epistle to the Romans	53
Appendix	91
Index	
Names	99
Words	100
Scriptural citations	104

Introduction

WHEN IN THE mid-390s Augustine turned his attention to the *Epistle to the Romans*, he was not encountering Paul for the first time. At several points in the preceding decade, both as a Manichaean "hearer" and later, in Italy, as a Catholic catechumen and budding Neoplatonist, he had had occasion to read Paul attentively.[1] But once back in Africa, before the watching eyes of his own church and its schismatic rival, the Donatists, Augustine had to confront publicly a well-organized Manichaean sect that based much of its dualist doctrine on a direct appeal to the New Testament, and especially to Paul.[2] Arguments against Manichaean determinism drawn largely from a philosophical defense of free will and individual virtue would be of little worth before such an audience, and such an enemy.[3] To reclaim Paul, Augustine had to make his case exegetically.[4]

The *Propositions from the Epistle to the Romans* and the *Unfinished Commentary on the Epistle to the Romans* are the fruit of this phase of Augustine's campaign against the Manichees, where he has to construct a synthetic, as well as polemical, reading of the Apostle. Here he takes the issue they have set (the origin of evil and the nature of man's will) and the hero they most used to support their claims (Paul), and develops a hermeneutic that emphasizes man's moral autonomy while preserving both the goodness of the Old Law and the gratuitous nature of God's grace.

Neither treatise is truly a finished piece. The *Propositions* is basically a reworked transcript of answers given in discussion with fellow clergymen who were having difficulty understanding Paul.[5] The formal commentary was never completed. Augustine became sidetracked by an issue arising in the course of his exegesis which he then pursued in a sermon. Returning to the commentary, he found himself "discouraged by the magnitude and labor of this task."[6] He never managed to continue this work beyond the first volume, in which he covered the opening phrases of Paul's greeting. But, though each is in its way unfinished, these two commentaries demonstrate Augustine's growing facility with this difficult Pauline text, and so provide an important perspective on his development as an exegete and theologian.

---

1. *Conf.* VII, xxi, 27.
2. See, e.g., *c. Fort.* 3; 7; 14; 17; and 18; cf. *Vita* VI.
3. As he had mounted, for example, in the Cassiciacum dialogues, in *de duabus animabus*, and in the first book of *de libero arbitrio*. A stern Biblicism was common cultural ground for both Catholics and Donatists, and even the Manichees evinced a conservative attitude toward the scriptural text. See P. Brown, *Augustine of Hippo*, pp. 42f.; 136.
4. Augustine turns to Paul continually in this decade to construct a non-dualistic anthropology and a response to the problem of evil. From 392 to c. 400 he produced *c. Fort.*, *Propp.*, *Expositio Epistolae ad Galatas*, *Inch. Ex.*, qu. 66-68 of *de 83 qu.*, and finally, capping this period, the *ad Simpl.* and the *Conf.*
5. *Retr.* I. 23 (22), 1.
6. *Retr.* I. 25 (24); cf. *Inch. Ex.* 14-23 and *Sermo* 71; Mt 12:32.

The interaction of human choice and divine influence presented here is much more complex and nuanced than in his earlier works, and he stresses the necessity of God's divine call and grace for salvation. But man, Augustine argues through *Romans*, himself earns salvation through the merit of freely willed faith—a position he will repudiate, again through *Romans*, scarcely two years later in the *ad Simplicianum*.

THE PROPOSITIONS

To understand *Romans*, Augustine begins, one must keep in mind the letter's main topic: the works of the Law and of grace. This immediately sets the stage for his anti-Manichaean exegesis, for Augustine (like Paul before him) must work hard to preserve the positive status of the Old Law and the role of human moral autonomy against those who (like the Manichees) see in Paul's statements a condemnation of both. To this end, he introduces the characteristic teaching of this treatise, the four stages of the history of salvation: before the Law, under the Law, under grace, and in peace.[7]

Before the Law, man is led heedlessly by his own appetites. The Law itself initiates the process of salvation by making man conscious of sin. His knowledge of sin, however, does not suffice to stop him from sinning; this comes only with the reception of grace, which is in Christ. But how then does man move from *sub lege* to *sub gratia*? Through the exercise of his free will. Man *sub lege* realizes that he has sinned; he thus chooses to respond in faith to God's call and so turns to Christ his Savior, who gives him grace. "For by his free will man has a means to believe in the Liberator and to receive grace so that, with the liberating assistance of him who gives it, man might cease to sin."[8] Having thus died to sin, the believer *sub gratia* has a foretaste of that eschatological peace to be shared with all the saints in the fourth stage, *in pace*, when at the body's resurrection man's nature will be changed from mortal to spiritual.

But the *Epistle to the Romans* relates two Old Testament episodes notoriously difficult to reconcile with a strong view of man's freedom: the choice of Jacob over Esau, 9:11–13; and the hardening of Pharaoh's heart, 9:17 (cf. Gen. 25: 21–23; Ex. 9:16). How is one to understand divine justice and human freedom, when God loved Jacob and hated Esau when both were still in the womb? By understanding divine prescience, Augustine answers. God foreknew that Jacob would respond in faith to his call, which Esau would spurn. So also with Pharaoh: his heart was indeed hardened, but justly, as punishment for his prior infidelity, which God had foreknown.[9] Augustine goes on to say what his argument in any case implied: election is

---

7. *Propp.* 13–18. Augustine first touched on this theme a few years earlier, commenting on Mt 14:16 in qu. 61, 7 of *de 83 qu.*
8. *Propp.* 44, 3.
9. See *Propp.* 61 for Jacob and Esau; *Propp.* 62 for Pharaoh.

based on merit, though not merit accruing from good works, an idea Paul explicitly refutes. Rather, one obtains merit by believing: *non opera sed fides inchoat meritum.*[10] There is no favoritism; everyone starts out equally sinful as from the same lump of clay, the same *massa* of humanity.[11] God justly elects those whom he foreknows will respond freely in faith to his call. God's call is the necessary precondition of man's salvation, but God issues this call on the basis of his foreknowledge of man's free decision. In this sense, then, man's free choice of faith determines his election.

THE UNFINISHED COMMENTARY

The *Unfinished Commentary* as a written work is both more diffuse and more coherent than the *Propositions.* In the course of his exegesis of the opening lines of *Romans,*[12] Augustine moves freely from Vergil to local anecdote through every epistle in the New Testament as he makes his major point: that God's gift of grace and peace is nothing other than the Holy Spirit, which is poured forth for all sinners that they might be released from sin and reconciled to God. But if God's love is so great and so generous, his mercy so abundant, then what, Augustine must ask, is the sin against the Holy Spirit which Christ said can never be forgiven?

Augustine proceeds to name and dismiss various possibilities. Sins of ignorance and sins of malice, sins committed either before or after baptism, adultery, treachery, murder—all these can be forgiven once the sinner repents. Pagans, Jews, heretics and schismatics, once they correct themselves, are all unhesitatingly pardoned and welcomed to the bosom of the Church. Even so great an adulterer as David, so great a maligner as Paul, once they repented, were cleansed of former sins. If forgiveness is denied to none of these great sinners once he repents, what, asks Augustine, can be the unpardonable sin? It is despair: "continuing in wickedness and maliciousness with despair of the kindness and mercy of God."[13] For to despair is to resist God's gift of the Holy Spirit, which brings peace and reconciliation. If the sinner despairs of forgiveness, he continues to sin, and so can never be forgiven. Again, this formulation puts great emphasis on man's autonomy. For despite God's call, his offer of grace, his demonstrations of mercy, and the witness of Christ's saving miracles, the sinner is still free to despair.

---

10. *Propp.* 62, 9; cf. *Retr.* 1. 23 (22), 3.
11. *Propp.* 62, 18-19. The concept of the *massa* will be crucial for Augustine's later teaching on Original Sin. It undergoes very rapid development in this period: cf. *Propp.* 62, 19; qu. 68, 3; *ad Simpl.* I. ii, 17ff.
12. Augustine aims to interpret the *textus,* almost the "literal sense" or "plain meaning" of Paul's letter; cf. his use of this term, again when discussing Paul, in *Conf.* VII, xxi, 27.
13. *Inch. Ex.* 22,3; cf. 14,1.

AUGUSTINE did not remain long with the exegetical solution to the problem of free will and grace that he had so painstakingly worked out in these commentaries. Returning to *Romans* 9 in the *ad Simplicianum*, he specifically repudiates his earlier argument that election turns upon God's foreknowledge of man's faith. Whereas formerly Augustine had held that man was free either to respond to God's call in faith and so repent, or to despair of mercy and so continue to sin, he now sees such autonomy as compromising divine omnipotence.[14] Man's good will, which Augustine had previously argued preceded God's call to initiate the merit of faith, is now itself elected by God; man's faith itself is not man's work but God's gift; and the righteousness of God, once incomparable to human justice because of its great mercy and the ubiquity of its grace, is now incomprehensible by reason of God's decision to remit to some inexplicably chosen few the universally owed debt of damnation.[15]

The importance of the *Propositions* and the *Unfinished Commentary*, then, lies less in the interpretation of *Romans* they propose—Augustine moves to his radically new position within two years—than in the conceptual vocabulary they enable him to absorb. From this point on, Augustine articulates a Christian anthropology against the Manichees that turns increasingly less on philosophical arguments *per se* and more on biblical, and especially Pauline, exegesis.[16] But if these commentaries represent a new phase in Augustine's anti-Manichaean polemic, they also mark the passing of his earlier view of divine influence and human freedom to a more somber reading of Paul, one that finds its most extreme expression, some thirty years later, in the controversy with Julian of Eclanum.

The interpretation of Paul Augustine works so hard to repudiate in the *ad Simplicanum* is not so much his enemies' as his own. It is in this sense that Augustine's early commentaries on *Romans* provide us with an oblique self-portrait, for it is here that we find articulated the silent half of that debate between Old and New Self that so informs his brilliant, melancholy response to Simplicianus, and whose portrait Augustine presents to us in the *Confessions*.

---

14. Cf. *Propp.* 55,4; *Inch. Ex.* 22,3; *ad Simpl.* I, ii, 13.
15. Cf. *Propp.* 13–18,12 and 13; 60,15; 62, 9; qu. 68, 4; *Inch. Ex.* 23,7; *ad Simpl.* I, ii, 5; *ad Simpl.* I, ii, 22, a complete reversal of his position in *Propp.* 44,3. For a more complete discussion, see P. Fredriksen, *Augustine's Early Interpretation of Paul* (Ph.D. diss., Princeton University, 1979) pp. 191–231.
16. Augustine's effort to defend Genesis against the Manichees had begun some years earlier with his allegorical *de Gen. c. Man.* (389). He began and forsook a literal commentary just before our period (*de Gen. ad litt. impf.*, in 393), and resumed his efforts in the following decade with the magisterial *de Genesi ad litteram* (c. 402–413).

THE TEXTS

Both Latin texts in the present work draw on three sources: Divjak's *CSEL* edition, Rousselet's review article, and my own reading of several manuscripts at the Bibliothèque Nationale, Paris and the Bodleian Library, Oxford.[17]

Divjak gives fifty-six manuscripts for the *Propositions*, from which he chose thirty to establish his text (pp. x–xi and p. 2). Among these he distinguishes two main branches: families *a*, *b*, and *c* derive from one, and family *d*, upon which he bases his text, derives from the other (p. xiv; for the stemma, see p. xxv).[18] Of the six manuscripts constituting *d*, I have studied *Codex Parisinus Latinus 1449 nouvelle acquisition*, 64r–72v, designated *A* by Divjak.[19] Written at Cluny in the 10th or 11th century, it contains numerous uncorrected scribal errors and many omissions (usually homoioteleuton), some of which are considerable (and many of which are not noted in Divjak's apparatus; see the Appendix, *infra*).

To establish the text of the *Unfinished Commentary*, Divjak chose ten from among the eighteen manuscripts listed in his preface (pp. xiii–xiv).[20] The manuscript tradition is so problematic that he does not attempt a stemma (pp. xxx–xxxi). I studied *O*, *Codex Oxoniensis Laud misc. 134*, 1r–14v. *O* is the oldest MS of this group (9th–10th c.), originating in the important Carolingian episcopal library at Wurzburg, a center for training scribes. This perhaps explains the MS's appearance, for it is a work of many hands, switching mid-folio and not infrequently mid-line.[21]

---

17. *Sancti Aureli Augustini Opera*, sect. VI, pars I. *Expositio quarundam propositionum ex Epistola ad Romanos. Epistolae ad Galatas Expositionis liber unus. Epistolae ad Romanos inchoata Expositio.* Recensuit Iohannes Divjak. *Corpus Scriptorum Ecclesiasticorum Latinorum*. Vol. LXXXIV, Vindobonae 1971; meticulously reviewed by Jean Rousselet, "A propos d'une édition critique: pour mieux lire les Commentaires d'Augustin sur les Epîtres aux Romains et aux Galates", *Revue des Etudes Augustiniennes*, xviii (1972) pp. 233–247.

18. Divjak's text agrees substantially with that given in the *Patrologia Latina*, vol. 35. Most differences tend to be limited to insignificant vocabulary and orthographical preferences (e.g., the *PL* almost invariably has *iis* where the *CSEL* has *his*), or minor variations in word order that do not effect the meaning. Rousselet points out that Rabanus Maur had worked with an exemplar very close to *d* (*art. cit.*, p. 234).

19. Also consulted were *O* = *Codex Parisinus Latinus 1975*, 1r–13v (9th c.) and *N* = *Codex Parisinus Latinus 17394*, 32r–48v (9th c.), both from family *a*; and *P* = *Codex Parisinus Latinus 12220*, 31v–50r (9th c.), from family *b*. For my text of these two commentaries I have maintained the traditional chapter divisions given in the *PL*, but have followed Divjak in numbering sentences.

20. He does not reveal his reasons for preferring one reading over another. Rousselet suggests, in light of the problematic MS tradition, that the coincidence of lessons *OTSEVU* be given authority (*art. cit.*, p. 237).

21. The most conservative count comes to at least five hands, three for the text and two for marginalia, chapter titles, punctuation, and corrections; a less conservative count could come to as many as twice that. For further discussion of this MS, see B. Bischoff's remarks, excerpted from his *Libri Sancti Kyliani*, in *Manuscripts at Oxford*, ed. A.C. de la Mare and B.C. Baker-Benfield (Bodleian, Oxford, 1980), p. 17.

Finally, for the English text, I have consulted volume XI of the *Oeuvres Complètes de Saint Augustin* (Paris, 1871) and the occasional passages given in Alexander Souter's *The Earliest Latin Commentaries of the Epistles of Saint Paul* (Oxford, 1927). The present translation, based on the text as I have edited it in light of Rousselet's suggestions and my own reading, is a complete revision of an earlier version which appeared as the appendix to my doctoral dissertation for Princeton University, *Augustine's Early Interpretation of Paul*.

I WOULD LIKE to thank the Department of History, University of California at Berkeley, for granting me the leave of absence which enabled me to consult European archives and to revise my earlier work; and also the Committee on Faculty Research at Berkeley, for its generous financial support of this project. Colleagues abroad and at home helped me at many points along the way. In Paris, Père Georges Folliet extended research privileges to me at the Institut des Etudes Augustiniennes, and Jean Rousselet discussed these treatises with me, suggesting more nuanced translations of several passages. Closer to home, my editor William R. Schoedel meticulously reviewed my English translation; Peter Brown and Fred Wakeman of the Berkeley history department read and criticized my introduction; Frank Derose of Berkeley's classics department suggested many important editorial changes in my Latin text; Jessica Coope assisted in preparing my manuscript for publication; and Jacqueline Craig of Berkeley's Office for History of Science and Technology, virtually my other editor, supervised production of the entire book. Closer still to home, my husband Richard Landes, by his personal example of dedication to his own work and his enthusiastic support of mine, aided and encouraged me throughout.

I dedicate this book with very great love to my grandmother, Sebastiana Poliofito Borrelli.

SELECT BIBLIOGRAPHY

For a verse-by-verse overview of Augustine's interpretations of *Romans*, see Karl Herman Schelkle, *Paulus: Lehrer des Väters* (Düsseldorf, 1956). Discussion of the theology and exegesis of these two commentaries may be found in Alexander Souter, *The Earliest Latin Commentaries on the Epistles of Saint Paul* (Oxford, 1927); Alberto Pincherle, *La formazione teologica di Sant'Agostino* (Rome, 1947); M. Löhrer, *Der Glaubensbegriff des hl. Augustins in seinen ersten Schriften bis zu den Confessiones* (Benzinger, 1955); and most recently, J. Patout Burns, *The Development of Augustine's Doctrine of Operative Grace* (Paris, 1980). For the personal and historical context of these writings, F. E. Cranz, "The development of Augustine's ideas on society before the Donatist Controversy," in R. A. Markus, *Augustine: a collection of critical essays* (New York, 1972); and Peter Brown, *Augustine of Hippo* (Berkeley, 1969). Auguste Luneau, *Histoire du Salut chez les Pères de l'Eglise. La Doctrine des âges du monde* (Paris, 1964) provides a good

introduction to Augustine's scheme of the four ages.

The most readily available texts of those other writings of Augustine's immediately relevant to these commentaries are: (i) for *de 83 diversis quaestionibus*, vol. X of the *Bibliothèque Augustinienne;* (ii) for the *ad Simplicianum*, vol. 44 of the *Corpus Christianorum, series Latina;* (iii) for the *Confessions*, the reprint of the 1934 Teubner text in *B.A.* vols. XIII–XIV; (iv) for the *Retractationes*, *B.A.* vol. XII. English translations may be found in these collections: *The Fathers of the Church* (New York, 1947–); *The Library of Christian Classics* (Philadelphia, 1953–55); *Ancient Christian Writers* (London, 1946–); and *Nicene and Post-Nicene Fathers*, first series, vols. I–VIII (reprinted Grand Rapids, 1974).

Abbreviations

SCRIPTURES

Eccles.	*Ecclesiastes*	Jms.	*James*
Ecclis.	*Ecclesiasticus* (Wisdom of Jesus ben Sirach)	Jn	*John*
Ex.	*Exodus*	1 Jn.	*1 John*
Gen.	*Genesis*	2 Jn.	*2 John*
Hos.	*Hosea*	3 Jn.	*3 John*
Is.	*Isaiah*	Lk	*Luke*
2 Sam.	*2 Samuel*	Mk	*Mark*
Sap.	*Sapientia* (Wisdom of Solomon)	Mt	*Matthew*
Prov.	*Proverbs*	1 Pet.	*1 Peter*
Ps.	*Psalms*	2 Pet.	*2 Peter*
Acts	*Acts of the Apostles*	Phil.	*Philippians*
Col.	*Colossians*	Rom.	*Romans*
1 Cor.	*1 Corinthians*	2 Thess.	*2 Thessalonians*
2 Cor.	*2 Corinthians*	1 Tim.	*1 Timothy*
Eph.	*Ephesians*	2 Tim.	*2 Timothy*
Gal.	*Galatians*	Tit.	*Titus*
Heb.	*Hebrews*		

AUGUSTINE'S WORKS

de Gen c. man.   *de Genesi contra Manichaeos*
                            (On Genesis, against the Manichees)

c. Fort.   *Acta contra Fortunatum Manichaeum*
                            (Debate with Fortunatus)

de Gen. ad litt. impf.   *de Genesi ad Litteram opus imperfectum*
                            (Unfinished Literal Commentary on Genesis)

Propp.   *Expositio quaraundum propositionum ex Epistola ad Romano.*
                            (Propositions from the Epistle to the Romans)

Inch. Ex.   *Epistolae ad Romanos inchoata expositio*
                            (Unfinished Commentary on the Epistle to the Romans)

de 83 qu.   *de 83 diversis quaestionibus*
                            (Answers to various questions)

ad Simpl.   *ad Simplicianum*

Conf.   *Confessiones*

Retr.   *Retractationes*

OTHER

Vita   Possidius, *Vita Sancti Augustini*
B.A.   Bibliothèque Augustinienne
CSEL   Corpus Scriptorum Ecclesiasticorum Latinorum
PL   Patrologia Latina

EXPOSITIO QUARUNDAM PROPOSITIONUM
EX EPISTOLA AD ROMANOS

**PROPOSITIONS FROM THE
EPISTLES TO THE ROMANS**

EXPOSITIO QUARUNDAM PROPOSITIONUM
EX EPISTOLA AD ROMANOS

Sensus hi sunt in epistola ad Romanos Pauli apostoli. Primo omnium ut quisque intelligat in hac epistola quaestionem versari operum legis et gratiae.

1. Quod autem dicit: *Secundum spiritum sanctificationis ex resurrectione mortuorum*, id est quia spiritus donum acceperunt post eius resurrectionem. Mortuorum vero resurrectionem memorat, quia in ipso omnes crucifixi sumus et resurreximus.

2. Quod autem dicit: *Ut gratiam vobis spiritualem impertiar*, dilectionem scilicet dei et proximi, ut per caritatem Christi gentibus in evangelium vocatis minime inviderent.

3. Quod autem dicit: *Revelatur ira dei de caelo super omnem impietatem* et cetera, ait et Salomon de sapientibus mundi: *Si enim tantum potuerunt scire ut possent aestimare saeculum, quomodo ipsius mundi dominum et creatorem non facilius invenerunt?* (2) Sed quos arguit Salomon non cognoverunt per creaturam creatorem, quos autem arguit apostolus cognoverunt sed gratias non egerunt et dicentes se esse sapientes stulti facti sunt et ad colenda simulacra deciderunt. (3) Nam sapientes gentium quod invenerint creatorem manifeste idem apostolus, cum Atheniensibus loqueretur, ostendit. (4) Cum enim dixisset quia: *in ipso vivimus et movemur et sumus*, addidit: *sicut et quidam secundum vos dixerunt.* (5) Hac autem intentione prius arguit impietatem gentium, ut ex hac probet etiam ad gratiam posse pertingere conversos. Iniustum est enim, ut poenam subeant impietatis et praemium fidei non accipiant.

4. Quod autem dicit: *Cognoscentes deum non ut deum glorificaverunt aut gratias egerunt,* hoc caput est peccati, de quo dictum est: *Initium omnis peccati superbia.* (2) Qui si gratias egissent deo, qui dederat hanc sapientiam, non sibi aliquid tribuissent cogitationibus suis. Quapropter in desideria cordis sui traditi sunt a domino, ut facerent quae non convenirent.

5. Quod autem dicit: *tradidit*, intelligitur, dimisit in desideria cordis illorum. Mercedem autem mutuam dicit recepisse de deo, ut traderentur in desideria cordis sui.

6. Quod autem demum dicit: *Tradidit illos deus in reprobam mentem* et cetera, *repletos* ait *omni iniquitate,* datur intelligi ad nocendum pertinere ista quae nunc dicit, id est facinora. (2) Superius autem dicebat de corruptelis, quae flagitia nominantur, ex quibus ad facinora pervenitur, quoniam quisque perniciosam dulcedinem flagitiorum sequens, dum impedientes personas removere conatur, pergit in facinus. (3) Sic distinctus est etiam ille locus in Sapientia Salomonis, ubi, cum

PROPOSITIONS FROM THE EPISTLES
TO THE ROMANS

These are the meanings of the ideas found in the letter of Paul the Apostle to the Romans. Above all else, one should understand that this letter addresses the question of the works of the Law and of grace.

1. "According to the Spirit of holiness by the resurrection of the dead" (Rom. 1:4), since the dead have received the gift of the Spirit following Christ's resurrection. But Paul mentions the resurrection of the dead because in Christ we have all been crucified and we have all been raised.

2. "So that I might impart to you spiritual grace" (1:11), namely, the love of God and neighbor, so that through the love of Christ they [Jewish Christians] might not in any way spurn those Gentiles called into the Gospel.

3. "The wrath of God is revealed from heaven against all impiety" and so on (1:18). Even Solomon said, concerning those whose wisdom is of this world, "If they could know so much that they could speculate about the universe, how did they not more easily discover the Lord of this world and its Creator?" (Sap. 13:9). (2) Those whom Solomon reproved had failed to know the Creator through his creation; but those whom the Apostle reproved knew but did not give thanks and, claiming to be wise, actually became fools and fell into idolatry. (3) For that the wise among the Gentiles had discovered the Creator, the Apostle himself plainly showed when he spoke to the Athenians. (4) For when he had said "In him we live and move and are," he added, "so even some of you have said" (Acts 17:28). (5) Thus he first reprimanded the Gentiles' impiety to show them that even they, once converted, could attain grace. For it would be unjust if they should incur the punishment for impiety but not receive the reward for faith.

4. "Knowing God, they neither honored him as God nor gave him thanks" (1:21). This is the source of sin, of which it has been said, "The beginning of all sin is pride" (Ecclis. 10:15). (2) If they had rendered thanks to God, who had given them this wisdom, they would not have given themselves any credit for their ideas. Wherefore the Lord handed them over to the desires of their own hearts, so that they did unseemly things.

5. "He handed them over" should be understood as God's abandoning them to their hearts' desires (1:24). For Paul says that they received a fitting reward from God, namely, that they were handed over to the desires of their *own* hearts.

6. Finally he says, "God handed them over to a debased mind," and so on, "and they were filled with every kind of wickedness" (1:28), that is, with those things that lead to wrongdoing of which he now speaks, namely, sinful acts. (2) For he had spoken above of those corruptions called lusts which lead to sinful acts. For whoever follows the pernicious sweetness of lusts, while striving to turn aside those people who impede him, proceeds into sin. (3) The *Wisdom of Solomon* also makes this distinction when,

enumerasset superiora flagitia, ait: *Circumveniamus pauperem iustum, quoniam inutilis est nobis* et cetera.

7-8. Quod autem dicit: *Non solum qui ea faciunt, sed etiam qui consentiunt facientibus,* significat quia quaecumque fecerunt non inviti fecerunt. Nam cum ad mala facta consentiunt, etiam illa, quae non fecerunt, approbant, et ideo de perfectis iam peccatis dicit: (2) *Propterea inexcusabilis es, o homo omnis qui iudicas. Omnis* autem cum dicit, subintrat iam ut monstret non solum gentilem sed etiam Iudaeum qui secundum legem volebat iudicare de gentibus.

9. Quod autem dicit: *Thesaurizas tibi iram in die irae,* iram dei ubique loquitur pro vindicta. Idcirco ait: *Iusti iudicii dei.* (2) Notandum autem quia ira dei ponitur et in novo testamento, quod, cum in vetere audiunt homines, qui legi veteri adversantur, culpandam eam putant, cum deus utique sicuti nos perturbationibus non subiaceat dicente Salomone: *Tu autem domine virtutum cum tranquillitate iudicas.* (3) Sed ira, ut dictum est, in vindictae significatione ponitur.

10. Quod autem dicit: *Contestante conscientia illorum,* secundum illum locum loquitur Iohannis apostoli, quo ait: *Dilectissimi, si cor nostrum nos reprehenderit, maior est deus conscientiae nostrae* et cetera.

11. Quod autem dicit: *spiritu, non littera,* hoc est, ut secundum spiritum, non secundum quod habet littera, lex intelligatur, quod utique contigit illis, qui circumcisionem magis carnaliter quam spiritualiter acceperunt.

12. Quod autem ait: *Cuius laus non ex hominibus sed ex deo,* illi convenit quod ait: *Qui in secreto Iudaeus est.*

13-18. Quod autem ait: *Quia non iustificabitur in lege omnis caro coram illo; per legem enim cognitio peccati* et cetera similia, quae quidam putant in contumeliam legis obicienda, sollicite satis legenda sunt, ut neque lex ab apostolo improbata videatur neque homini arbitrium liberum sit ablatum. (2) Itaque quattuor istos gradus hominis distinguamus: ante legem, sub lege, sub gratia, in pace. Ante legem sequimur concupiscentiam carnis, sub lege trahimur ab ea, sub gratia nec sequimur eam nec trahimur ab ea, in pace nulla est concupiscentia carnis. (3) Ante legem ergo non pugnamus, quia non solum concupiscimus et peccamus, sed etiam approbamus peccata. Sub lege pugnamus sed vincimur. Fatemur enim mala esse quae facimus, et fatendo mala esse utique nolumus facere, sed, quia nondum est gratia, superamur. (4) In isto gradu ostenditur nobis, quomodo iaceamus, et, dum surgere volumus et cadimus, gravius affligimur. (5) Inde hic dicitur: *Lex subintravit, ut abundaret delictum.* Inde et quod nunc positum est: *Per legem enim cognitio peccati.* Non enim ablatio peccati est,

having enumerated the aforementioned lusts, it says: "Let us ensnare the poor just man, for he stands in our way" (Sap. 2:12).

7-8. "Not only those who commit such acts, but also those who consent to others doing them" (1:32), means that whatever they had done they did willingly. For when they consented to the evil deeds of others, they approved even those deeds they did not actually do themselves. And so Paul speaks of already-accomplished sins when he says: (2) "Therefore you are without excuse, every man who judges" (2:1). Moreover, when he says "every man," he introduces an indictment not only of the Gentile but also of the Jew, who wished to judge the Gentiles according to the Law.

9. "You are storing up wrath for yourself on the Day of Wrath" (2:5). Every time Paul speaks of the wrath of God he means it in the sense of punishment. For that reason he adds, "of the just judgment of God." (2) One should also note that the "wrath of God" stands even in the New Testament, because when those men who are hostile to the Old Law hear this in the Old Testament, they think it must be censured, since God is not at all, as we are, subject to perturbation. As Solomon says, "You, O Lord of Hosts, judge in tranquility" (Sap. 12:18). (3) But wrath, as I have said, occurs here in the sense of punishment.

10. "By their conflicting thoughts" (2:15). This accords with the apostle John when he says, "Dearly beloved, if our own hearts should condemn us, God is greater than our conscience" (1 Jn. 3:20).

11. "By the spirit, not the letter" (2:29). That is, the Law should be understood in a spiritual, not literal, sense. This pertains especially to those who have understood circumcision in a fleshly rather than spiritual way.

12. "His praise is not from men, but God" (2:29), accords with Paul's statement, "He who is a Jew inwardly."

13-18. "For no flesh will be justified before him by the Law, for through the Law comes knowledge of sin" (3:20), and other such things which, some think, must be intended as a reproach to the Law. Such statements must be read with great care, so that the Apostle seems neither to condemn the Law nor to take away man's free will. (2) Therefore, let us distinguish these four stages of man: prior to the Law; under the Law; under grace; and in peace. Prior to the Law, we pursue fleshly concupiscence; under the Law, we are pulled by it; under grace, we neither pursue nor are pulled by it; in peace, there is no concupiscence of the flesh. (3) Therefore prior to the Law we do not struggle, because not only do we lust and sin, but we even assent to sin. Under the Law we struggle but we are overcome. We admit that we do evil, and by that admission, that we really do not want to do it, but because we still lack grace we are overwhelmed. (4) In this stage we learn how low we lie, and when we want to rise and yet we fall, we are the more gravely afflicted. (5) Whence Paul in this letter says, "The Law was introduced that sin might abound" (5:20), and at this point notes that, "through the Law comes knowledge of sin" (3:20), but not the removal of

quia per solam gratiam aufertur peccatum. (6) Bona ergo lex, quia ea vetat quae vetanda sunt et ea iubet quae iubenda sunt. Sed cum quisque illam viribus suis se putat implere, non per gratiam liberatoris sui, nihil ei prodest ista praesumptio, immo etiam tantum nocet, ut et
5 vehementiore peccandi desiderio rapiatur et in peccatis etiam praevaricator inveniatur. (7) *Ubi enim non est lex, nec praevaricatio.* Sic ergo iacens, cum se quisque cognoverit per seipsum surgere non valere, imploret liberatoris auxilium. Venit ergo gratia, quae donet peccata praeterita et conantem adiuvet et tribuat caritatem iustitiae et auferat
10 metum. (8) Quod cum fit, tametsi desideria quaedam carnis, dum in hac vita sumus, adversus spiritum nostrum pugnant, ut eum ducant in peccatum, non tamen his desideriis consentiens spiritus, quoniam est fixus in gratia et caritate dei, desinit peccare. (9) Non enim in ipso desiderio pravo, sed in nostra consensione peccamus. Ad hoc valet,
15 quod dicit idem apostolus: *Non ergo regnet peccatum in vestro mortali corpore ad oboediendum desideriis eius.* (10) Hinc enim ostendit esse desideria, quibus non oboediendo peccatum in nobis regnare non sinimus. Sed quoniam ista desideria de carnis mortalitate nascuntur, quae trahimus ex primo peccato primi hominis, unde carnaliter nas-
20 cimur, non finientur haec nisi resurrectione corporis immutationem illam, quae nobis promittitur, meruerimus, ubi perfecta pax erit, cum in quarto gradu constituemur. (11) Ideo autem perfecta pax, quia nihil nobis resistet non resistentibus deo. Hoc est quod dicit apostolus: *Corpus quidem mortuum est propter peccatum, spiritus autem vita est propter*
25 *iustitiam. Si ergo spiritus eius qui suscitavit Iesum a mortuis habitat in vobis, qui suscitavit Iesum Christum a mortuis vivificabit et mortalia corpora vestra per inhabitantem spiritum eius in vobis.* (12) Liberum ergo arbitrium perfecte fuit in primo homine, in nobis autem ante gratiam non est liberum arbitrium ut non peccemus, sed tantum ut peccare nolimus.
30 Gratia vero efficit, ut non tantum velimus recte facere, sed etiam possimus, non viribus nostris sed liberatoris auxilio, qui nobis etiam perfectam pacem in resurrectione tribuet, quae pax perfecta bonam voluntatem consequitur. (13) *Gloria* enim *in excelsis deo et in terra pax hominibus bonae voluntatis.*

35 **19.** Quod autem dicit: *Legem ergo evacuamus per fidem? Absit. Sed legem statuimus,* id est, firmamus. Sed quemadmodum firmanda erat lex nisi per iustitiam? (2) Iustitiam autem quae est ex fide, quia ea ipsa quae non poterant impleri per legem, per fidem impleta sunt.

20. Quod autem ait: *Si enim Abraham ex operibus iustificatus est,*
40 *habet gloriam, sed non apud deum,* hoc est, quia Abraham sine lege dum non ex operibus legis gloriam conquirit, quasi suis viribus legem impleat, cum adhuc lex ista data non esset, dei illa gloria, non sua est. (2) Non enim merito sui tamquam ex operibus, sed dei gratia fide iustificatus est.

sin, which comes through grace alone. (6) Therefore the Law is good, for it forbids what ought to be forbidden and prescribes what ought to be prescribed. But when anyone thinks that he can fulfill the Law by his own strength and not through the grace of his Savior, this presumption does him no good. Rather it so harms him that he is both seized by a stronger desire to sin, and by his sins is made a transgressor. (7) For "where the Law is not, neither is there trespass" (4:15). Therefore let the man lying low, when he realizes that he cannot rise by himself, implore the aid of the Liberator. For then comes grace, which pardons earlier sins and aids the struggling one, adds charity to justice, and takes away fear. (8) When this happens, even though certain fleshly desires fight against our spirit while we are in this life, to lead us into sin, nonetheless our spirit resists them because it is fixed in the grace and love of God, and ceases to sin. (9) For we sin not by having this perverse desire but by consenting to it. Relevant here is what the same Apostle says: "Do not let sin reign in your mortal bodies, so that you obey its desires" (6:12). (10) Thus here he shows we still have desires but, by not obeying them, that we do not allow sin to reign in us. But these desires arise from the mortality of the flesh, which we bear from the first sin of the first man, whence we are born fleshly. Thus they will not cease save at the resurrection of the body, when we will have merited that transformation promised to us. Then there will be perfect peace, when we have been established in the fourth stage. (11) Perfect peace, since nothing will resist us who do not resist God. This is what the Apostle says: "Indeed, the body is dead because of sin, but the spirit is life because of righteousness. If then the spirit of him who raised Jesus from the dead lives in you, he who raised Christ Jesus from the dead will give life even to your mortal bodies also through his spirit dwelling within you" (8:10–11). (12) For free will existed perfectly in the first man; we, however, prior to grace, do not have free will so as not to sin, but only so much that we do not want to sin. But with grace, not only do we want to act rightly, but we can; not by our own strength, but by the help of the Liberator. And at the resurrection he will bring us that perfect peace which follows from good will. (13) For "Glory to God in the highest, and on earth peace to men of good will" (Lk 2:14).

19. "Do we then cancel the Law by this faith? By no means! Rather, we establish it" (3:31), that is, we affirm it. But how ought the Law be affirmed, if not by righteousness? (2)—a righteousness, moreover, that exists by faith, for those things which could not be fulfilled through the Law were fulfilled through faith.

20. "For if Abraham was justified by works, he has something to boast about, but not before God" (4:2). That is, since Abraham without the Law acquired glory not through the works of the Law (as if by his own strength he could fulfill the Law) since that Law was not yet given, the glory is God's, not his. (2) For he was justified not by his own merit as though through works, but by the grace of God through faith.

21. Quod autem ait: *Ei autem qui operatur, merces non imputatur secundum gratiam sed secundum debitum,* dixit, quemadmodum homines hominibus reddant mercedem. (2) Nam deus per gratiam dedit, quia peccatoribus dedit, ut per fidem iuste viverent, id est, bene operarentur. Quod ergo bene operamur iam accepta gratia, non nobis sed illi tribuendum est, qui per gratiam nos iustificavit. (3) Nam si debitam mercedem vellet reddere, poenam redderet debitam peccatoribus.

22. Quod autem ait: *Qui justificat impium,* hoc est ex impio pium facit, ut de cetero in ipsa pietate permaneat atque justitia, quia ideo justificatus est ut iustus sit, non ut peccare sibi licere arbitretur.

23. Quod autem ait: *Lex enim iram operatur* vindictam significat et ad illum secundum gradum pertinet, cum est quisque sub lege.

24. Quod autem ait: *Ante deum cui credidit,* significavit fidem in interiore homine esse in conspectu dei, non in ostentatione hominum, sicuti est carnis circumcisio.

25. Quod autem ait de Abraham: *Dans gloriam deo,* adversus illos positum est, qui gloriam suam de operibus legis coram hominibus quaerebant.

26. Quod autem ait: *Non solum autem, sed et gloriamur in tribulationibus* et cetera, gradatim perducit usque ad caritatem dei, quam caritatem dicit nos habere per donum spiritus; monstrat illa omnia, quae possemus nobis tribuere, deo esse tribuenda, qui spiritum sanctum per gratiam dare dignatus est.

27–28. Quod autem ait: *Usque ad legem enim peccatum in mundo fuit,* intelligendum est, quousque veniret gratia. (2) Contra eos enim dictum est, qui arbitrantur per legem auferri potuisse peccata. Dicit enim apostolus manifestata esse peccata per legem, non autem ablata cum dicit: *Peccatum autem non deputabatur cum lex non esset.* Non enim ait: non erat, sed: *non deputabatur.* (3) Neque cum lex data est, ablatum est, sed deputari coepit, id est, apparere. Non ergo putemus usque ad legem ita dictum esse, quasi iam sub lege non esset peccatum, sed dictum est sic: *usque ad legem,* ut totum legis tempus adnumeres usque ad finem legis, quod est Christus.

29. Quod autem ait: *Sed regnavit mors ab Adam usque ad Moysen et in his qui non peccaverunt in similitudinem praevaricationis Adae,* duobus modis distinguitur: aut *in similitudinem praevaricationis Adae regnavit mors,* quia et qui non peccaverunt, ex origine mortalitatis Adam mortui sunt; aut certe: (2) *Regnavit mors et in his, qui non in similitudinem praevaricationis Adae peccaverunt,* sed ante legem peccaverunt, ut illi peccasse intelligantur in similitudinem praevaricationis Adae, qui legem acceperunt, quia et Adam accepta praecepti lege peccavit. (3) Sane etiam id quod

21. "For one who works, his wages are not reckoned to him as a gift, but as his due" (4:4). Paul here spoke of the way men give wages to men. (2) For God gave by grace, since he gave to sinners, so that by faith they might live justly, that is, do good works. Therefore the good works we do once we have received grace are due not to ourselves, but to him who justified us by grace. (3) For if he had wanted to pay a just wage, he would have meted out punishment, the wage owed to sinners.

22. "Who justifies the impious" (4:5), that is, he makes the impious man pious so that in the future the man might persevere in this very piety and righteousness. For a man is justified that he might be just, not that he might suppose he is permitted to continue to sin. (Cf. 6.1f.).

23. "For the Law works wrath" (4:15), which means punishment. This pertains to that second stage, when all are under the Law.

24. "In the presence of God in whom he believed" (4:17) means that faith is in the inner man, in the sight of God, and not in the displays of men, like fleshly circumcision.

25. Concerning Abraham he says: "giving glory to God" (4:20), against those who were seeking their own glory in the sight of men by the works of the Law.

26. "More than that, we glory in our sufferings" (5:3) and so on, so that gradually he leads us to the love of God (5:6), which he says we have through the gift of the Spirit. Paul shows us that all those things which we might attribute to ourselves ought to be attributed to God, who deigned to give us the Holy Spirit through grace.

27-28. "Up to the time of the Law sin was in the world" (5:13), meaning up until the time that grace came. (2) He said this against those who thought that sin could be taken away through the Law. For the Apostle states that sins are made manifest by the Law, not abolished, when he says, "Sin was not reckoned when there was no Law" (5:13). He does not say "Sin was not," but, "it was not reckoned." (3) Nor once the Law was given was sin taken away, but it began to be reckoned, that is, it became evident. Nor should we take the phrase "up until the time of the Law" to mean that already under the Law there was no sin. But he says "until the Law" so that you would count the whole time of the Law up to the end of the Law, which is Christ.

29. "But death reigned from Adam to Moses, even over those who did not sin in the likeness of Adam's transgression" (5:14). This can be punctuated in two ways: "in the likeness of Adam's transgression, death reigned," since even those who did not sin still died because of their origin in the mortality of Adam; or surely: (2) "Death reigned, even over those who did not sin in the likeness of Adam's transgression," but sinned before the time of the Law. Thus they who did receive the Law may be understood to have sinned in the likeness of Adam's transgression, because Adam also sinned after having received the law of the command. (3) Of

dictum est: *usque ad Moysen,* totum tempus legis intelligendum est. illum mors, sic per dominum nostrum vita. (4) Quod autem ait: *Sed non sicut delictum, ita est et donatio,* duobus modis donatio praecellit: vel quod multo magis abundat gratia, quia utique in aeternum per illam vivitur, temporaliter autem per mortem Adae mors regnavit; vel quod unius delicti condemnatione mors multorum facta est per Adam, per dominum autem nostrum Iesum Christum multorum delictorum donatione data gratia in vitam aeternam. (5) Aliam vero differentiam sic explicat dicens: *Et non sicut per unum peccantem ita est et donum. Nam iudicium quidem ex uno in condemnationem, gratia autem ex multis delictis ad iustificationem.* (6) Ex uno ergo quod dictum est, subauditur delicto, quia sequitur: *gratia autem ex multis delictis.* Ergo haec differentia est, quod in Adam unum delictum damnatum est, a domino autem multa donata sunt. (7) Quod ergo sequitur, ambas istas differentias tenet, ut explicetur sic: *Si enim ob unius delictum mors regnavit per unum, multo magis qui abundantiam gratiae et iustitiae accipiunt, in vita regnabunt per unum Iesum Christum.* (8) Quod ergo dixit: *Multo magis regnabunt,* ad vitam aeternam pertinet, quod autem dixit: *Abundantiam gratiae accipiunt,* ad donationem multorum delictorum pertinet. (9) Post explicatas autem has differentias, redit ad formam unde coeperat, cuius ordinem suspenderat, cum diceret: *Sicut enim per unum hominem peccatum intravit in hunc mundum et per peccatum mors.* (10) Ad quod nunc redit, cum dicit: *Itaque sicut per unius delictum in omnes homines ad condemnationem, ita et per unius iustificationem in omnes homines ad iustificationem vitae. Sicut enim per inoboedientiam unius hominis peccatores constituti sunt multi, ita et per unius oboedientiam iusti constituentur multi.* (11) Haec est forma futuri Adam, de qua superius loqui coeperat et eius aliquas differentias interponens distulerat ordinem, ad quem nunc redeundo conclusit dicens: *Itaque sicut per unius delictum in omnes homines* et cetera.

30. Quod autem ait: *Lex subintravit, ut abundaret delictum,* ipso verbo satis significavit nescisse Iudaeos, qua dispensatione lex data sit. (2) Non enim data est, quae possit vivificare, quia gratia vivificat per fidem, sed data est lex ad ostendendum quantis quamque arctis vinculis peccatorum constricti tenerentur qui de suis viribus ad implendam iustitiam praesumebant. (3) Sic abundavit peccatum, cum et concupiscentia ex prohibitione ardentior facta est et peccantibus contra legem praevaricationis crimen accessit. Quod intelligit, qui secundum gradum in illis quattuor gradibus considerat.

31. Quod autem ait: *Quid ergo dicemus? Permanebimus in peccato, ut gratia abundet? Absit. Qui mortui sumus peccato, quomodo vivemus in eo?* hinc ostendit de praeteritis peccatis factum esse, ut donarentur, et in eo superabundasse gratiam, ut praeterita peccata dimitterentur. (2) Ergo quisquis adhuc quaerit augmenta peccati, ut augmentum

course, by the phrase "until Moses" one understands the whole time of the Law. Moreover, Adam is "the figure of the one who was to come," but antithetically, for as death came through him, so through our Lord came life. (4) "But the free gift is not like the trespass" (5:15), for the gift excels in two ways. First, grace abounds much more in that it grants eternal life, although for the time being, through the death of Adam, death reigns. Second, by the condemnation of one transgression Adam caused the death of many, but by the gift for many sins our Lord Jesus Christ has given grace for life eternal. (5) And thus Paul explains another distinction, saying: "The gift is not like the effects of that one sinner. For the judgment following from one led to condemnation, but grace following from many trespasses, to justification" (5:16). (6) "From one" should be understood as "from one trespass," since "grace from many trespasses" follows. This, then, is the distinction: in Adam one sin was condemned, but by the Lord many sins were forgiven. (7) What follows maintains both these different senses, as Paul explains: "For if on account of one man's sin death reigned through one man, how much more will those who receive the abundance of grace and righteousness reign in life through one man Jesus Christ" (5:17). (8) Thus "how much more will they reign" pertains to life eternal; "they receive the abundance of grace," to the forgiveness of many sins. (9) Having drawn these distinctions, Paul returns to his initial outline, whose order he had interrupted when he said, "For just as through one man sin entered into the world and death through sin." (10) He now goes back to his point. "And so just as through one man's transgression all men were brought to condemnation, so through one man's righteousness all men were brought to the justification of life. For as through one man's disobedience many men were made sinners, so through one man's obedience many men will be made righteous" (5:18-19). This is the figure of the future Adam, which he had begun to speak of above. Interrupting his sequence of thought by introducing these two distinctions, he concludes by returning now to his point, "and thus through the transgression of one man all men" etc.

30. "The Law entered in to increase the trespass" (5:20). By this very expression Paul sufficiently indicated that the Jews did not understand why the Law had been given. (2) It was not to bring life, for grace does this through faith. But the Law was given to show what great and tight bonds of sins bound those who presumed to attain righteousness by their own strength. (3) Thus sin abounded, as both the prohibition made concupiscence more ardent, and the offense of trespass attended those who sinned against the Law. He who calls to mind the second of the four stages of man understands this.

31. "What then shall we say? Shall we continue in sin, that grace might abound? By no means! How shall we who have died to sin live in it?" (6:1-2). Here Paul makes a point about past sins: they have been pardoned, and in this pardon grace superabounded, so that earlier sins were dismissed. (2) Therefore anyone seeking to increase sin in order to feel an

gratiae sentiat, non intelligit id se agere, ut nihil in eo gratia operetur. Opus enim gratiae est, ut moriamur peccato.

32-34. Quod autem ait: *Hoc scientes, quia vetus homo noster simul crucifixus est, ut evacuaretur corpus peccati,* refertur ad illud, quod per Moysen dictum est: *Maledictus omnis, qui in ligno perpenderit.* (2) Veteris enim hominis crucifixio significata est in cruce domini, sicut novi hominis instauratio in resurrectione significata est. (3) Manifestum est autem secundum eum nos agere veterem hominem, qui maledictus est. Propter quem peccatum et de domino dictum esse nemo ambigit, quod peccata nostra portavit et peccatum pro nobis fecit et de peccato condemnavit peccatum. (4) Quid est autem evacuare corpus peccati? Ipse exposuit: *Ut ultra non serviamus peccato,* et illud quod ait: *Si mortui sumus cum Christo,* hoc est, si crucifixi sumus cum Christo. (5) Dicit enim alio loco: *Qui enim Christi Iesu sunt, carnem suam crucifixerunt cum vitiis et concupiscentiis.* Non ergo domino maledixit Moyses, sed, quid ostenderet eius crucifixio, prophetavit.

35. Quod autem ait: *Peccatum enim in vobis non dominabitur: non enim estis sub lege, sed sub gratia,* utique ad tertium illum gradum iam pertinet, ubi homo iam mente servit legi dei, quamvis carne serviat legi peccati. Non enim obaudit desiderio peccati quamvis adhuc sollicitent concupiscentiae et provocent ad consensionem, donec vivificetur etiam corpus et absorbeatur mors in victoriam. (2) Quia ergo non consentimus desideriis pravis, in gratia sumus et non regnat peccatum in nostro mortali corpore; et omnino ex illo loco, ubi ait: *Qui mortui sumus peccato, quomodo vivemus in eo?* eum describit, qui est sub gratia constitutus. Cui autem dominatur peccatum, quamvis velit peccato resistere, adhuc sub lege est, nondum sub gratia.

36. Quod autem dicit: *Mulier enim sub viro, vivo marito, vincta est legi; si autem mortuus fuerit vir eius, evacuata est a lege viri* et cetera, animadvertendum est istam similitudinem in hoc differre ab ea re, propter quam adhibita est, quod hic virum dicit mori, ut mulier nubat cui volet liberata utique a lege viri; (2) ibi autem cum constituat animam quasi mulierem, virum autem quasi passiones peccatorum, quae operantur in membris, ut fructum ferant morti, id est, ut tali coniugio proles digna nascatur, et lex, quae data est non ad auferendum peccatum vel ad liberationem a peccato, sed ad ostendendum peccatum ante gratiam, per quod factum est ut sub lege positi vehementiore desiderio peccandi raperentur et amplius etiam praevaricatione peccarent—(3) cum ergo et ibi tria sint, anima tamquam mulier, passiones peccatorum tamquam vir et lex tamquam lex viri, non ibi tamen peccatis mortuis tamquam viro mortuo liberari animam dicit, sed ipsam animam mori peccato et liberari a lege, ut sit

increase of grace does not understand that he so conducts himself that grace has accomplished nothing in him. For the work of grace is that we might die to sin.

32-34. "We know that our old man was crucified at the same time, in order to cancel the body of sin" (6:6) refers to what Moses said, "Cursed be every man hanged from a tree" (Deut. 21:23). (2) For as the crucifixion of the old man was symbolized by the cross of the Lord, so the renewal of the new man was signified by the resurrection. (3) Clearly for Paul we are in the role of the old man who is accursed, on whose behalf, as no one doubts, the Lord himself was called "sin," because "he bore our sins" (cf. Jn 1:29; 1 Pt. 2:24), and "he made sin for us" (cf. 2 Cor. 5:21), and "by sin condemned sin" (Rom. 8:3). (4) And what does Paul mean by "to cancel the body of sin"? He explained himself: "that we might serve sin no more," and: "If we have died with Christ..." that is, if we have been crucified with Christ. (5) As he says elsewhere, "Those who are of Christ Jesus have crucified their flesh with its vices and appetites" (Gal. 5:24). Therefore Moses did not malign the Lord, but prophesied what his crucifixion would signify.

35. "Sin will have no dominion over you, for you are not under the Law, but under grace" (6:14). This clearly refers to that third stage when man in his mind now serves the Law of God, even though his flesh serves the law of sin (cf. 7:25). For he does not obey the urge of sin, even though lusts will still trouble him and seek his consent until the body is raised and death is swallowed up in victory (1 Cor. 15:54). (2) Thus because we do not consent to depraved longings, we are under grace, and sin does not reign in our mortal bodies. Indeed, here where Paul says, "How shall we who have died to sin still live in it?" he describes the man who is established in grace. But man who is dominated by sin, even though he wants to resist it, is still under the Law and not yet under grace.

36. "The married woman is bound by the Law under her husband as long as he lives; but if her husband dies, she is discharged from the law of her husband" (7:2). One should note how this analogy differs from its subject. For here Paul states that the husband dies, so that the woman may marry whom she will, since she has been freed entirely from the law of her husband. (2) Moreover, there when he designates the soul as the woman, and her husband as the passions of the sins that work in the members to produce the fruit of death, so that offspring are born worthy of such a union (cf. 7:4-6), and the Law, which was given not to take away sin nor to free man from sin but to reveal sin before grace, which is why those under the Law are seized by a more violent desire to sin, and sin all the more because of the trespass—(3) when therefore he makes this triple analogy—the soul symbolized by the wife, the passions of sin by the husband, and the Law by the law of the husband—Paul does not say that the soul is freed when sins are dead as the wife is freed when her husband is dead. Rather, he says that the soul itself dies to sin and is freed from the Law, so that it might

alterius viri, id est Christi, cum mortua fuerit peccato quamvis adhuc quasi vivente ipso peccato. (4) Quod fit, cum adhuc manentibus in nobis desideriis et incitamentis quibusdam ad peccandum non oboedimus tamen neque consentimus mente servientes legi dei, quia
5 mortui sumus peccato. (5) Morietur autem et peccatum, cum reformatio corporis in resurrectione facta fuerit, de qua post dicit: *Vivificabit et mortalia corpora vestra propter spiritum manentem in vobis.*

37. Quod autem dicit: *Occasione autem accepta peccatum per mandatum operatum est in me omnem concupiscentiam,* intelligendum est non
10 omnem fuisse concupiscentiam, antequam prohibitione aucta esset. (2) Augetur enim prohibitione concupiscentia, quando deest gratia liberantis; ideo nondum est omnis, antequam prohibeatur. (3) Cum autem prohibita fuerit desistente, ut diximus, gratia, tantum crescit concupiscentia, ut ita in suo genere omnis, id est, consummata fiat, ut
15 etiam contra legem fiat et praevaricatione crimen accumulet. (4) Quod autem dicit: *Sine lege enim peccatum mortuum est,* non, quia non est, dixit, *mortuum est,* sed quia latet, quod in consequentibus manifestat, cum dicit: *Sed peccatum, ut appareat peccatum, per bonum mihi operatum est mortem.* (5) Bona est enim lex, sed sine gratia tantummodo osten-
20 dit peccata, non tollit.

38. Quod autem ait: *Ego autem vivebam aliquando sine lege,* intelligendum est, vivere mihi videbar, quia ante mandatum latebat peccatum. (2) Et quod ait: *Adveniente autem mandato peccatum revixit, ego autem mortuus sum,* intelligendum est, peccatum apparere coepit, ego
25 autem mortuum me esse cognovi.

39. Quod autem ait: *Peccatum enim occasione accepta per mandatum fefellit me et per illud occidit,* ideo dictum est, quia desiderii prohibiti fructus dulcior est. (2) Unde etiam, quaecumque peccata occulte fiunt, dulciora sunt, quamvis mortifera ista dulcedo sit. Inde est, quod apud
30 Salomonem fallacis doctrinae imagine sedens mulier et invitans, ut ad se veniant insipientes, scribitur dicere: *Panes occultos libenter edite et aquam dulcem furtivam bibite.* (3) Ista dulcedo est occasio per mandatum inventa peccati, quae cum appetitur, utique fallit et in maiores amaritudines vertit.

35 **40.** Quod autem ait: *Quod ergo bonum est, mihi factum est mors? Absit. Sed peccatum, ut appareat peccatum, per bonum mihi operatum est mortem,* hic evidenter ostendit, quod superius dixerat: (2) *Sine lege enim peccatum mortuum est,* ideo dixisse, quia latet, quandoquidem nunc dixit non illud bonum, id est, legem factum sibi esse mortem, sed peccatum
40 operatum esse mortem per bonum legis, id est, ut appareret peccatum,

belong to another husband, i.e., Christ, since the soul has died to sin, though sin itself, as it were, still lives. (4) This happens when, although desires and certain incitements to sin remain, we neither obey nor consent to them, for in our minds we serve the Law of God, because we have died to sin. (5) Moreover sin too will die when the body is transformed at the resurrection, concerning which Paul later says, "He will bring life again to your mortal bodies, because of the Spirit dwelling within you" (8:11).

37. "Sin, finding opportunity in the commandment, wrought in me every sort of concupiscence" (7:8). One should understand that every sort of concupiscence did not exist until prohibition increased it. (2) For since prohibition increases concupiscence in the absence of the Liberator's grace, before prohibition therefore every sort of concupiscence did not exist. (3) But when the prohibition was laid down, as we have said, in the absence of grace, concupiscence grew so greatly that it became complete—that is, consummate—in its nature, so much so that it even came against the Law, piling criminal offense on top of transgression. (4) When Paul says, "Without the Law sin lies dead" (7:8), he did not mean that sin does not exist, but that it lies hidden. His following statement makes this clear when he says, "But sin, in order to appear as sin, worked death in me through what is good" (7:13). (5) For the Law is good, but without grace it only reveals sins, and does not take them away.

38. "I was once alive apart from the Law" (7:9) should be understood to mean, 'I seemed to be alive', since before the command sin lay hidden. (2) "With the coming of the command, sin revived and I died" (7:10), that is, sin began to make itself known, and moreover I came to recognize that I was dead.

39. "For sin, finding the opportunity in the commandment, deceived me and so through it slew me" (7:11) because the fruit of a prohibited desire is sweeter. (2) Whence sins committed in secret are sweeter, even though that sweetness is deadly. Thus the seated woman in the Proverbs of Solomon, the image of false doctrine inviting the senseless to come to her, says, "Eat hidden bread willingly, and drink stolen waters which are sweet" (Prov. 9:17).[1] (3) This sweetness is the opportunity of sin found in the commandment (cf. 8:8) which, when sought, deceives utterly and turns into great bitterness.

40. "Did that which is good become death for me? By no means! But sin, to appear as sin, wrought death in me through what is good" (7:13). Paul here clarifies his earlier statement, (2) "without the Law sin lies dead." He had said this because sin lay hidden, as he now says not that a good thing (that is, the Law) had become death for him, but that sin wrought death through the good of the Law, thereby becoming manifest where,

---

1. Augustine first makes this association in *de Gen c. Man.* II.41; cf. *Conf.* III.vi, 11, where the woman is specifically equated with the Manichees.

quod latebat sine lege. (3) Tunc enim se mortuum quisque cognoscit, cum illud, quod recte praeceptum esse confitetur, implere non potest, et praevaricationis crimine amplius peccat, quam si non prohiberetur. (4) Hoc est, quod in consequentibus dicit: *Ut fiat supra modum peccator aut peccatum per mandatum,* quod ante mandatum minus erat, quia, ubi non est lex, nec praevaricatio.

41. Quod autem ait: *Scimus quia lex spiritualis est, ego autem carnalis sum,* satis ostendit non posse impleri legem nisi a spiritualibus, quales facit gratia dei. (2) Similis enim quisque factus ipsi legi facile implet, quod praecipit, nec erit sub illa sed cum illa; is est autem, qui iam non capitur temporalibus bonis nec terretur temporalibus malis.

42. Quod autem ait: *Venumdatus sub peccato,* intelligendum est, quod unusquisque peccando animam suam diabolo vendit accepta tamquam pretio dulcedine temporalis voluptatis. (2) Unde et dominus noster redemptor dictus est, quia hoc modo, quo dictum est, venditi eramus.

43. Quod autem ait: *Quod enim operor, ignoro,* potest videri minus intelligentibus contrarium esse illi sententiae, qua dixit: *Peccatum, ut appareat peccatum, per bonum mihi operatum est mortem.* Quomodo enim apparet, si ignoratur? (2) Sed ignoro sic dictum est hoc loco, ut intelligatur, non approbo. Quomodo enim tenebrae non videntur, sed lucis comparatione sentiuntur—hoc est autem sentire tenebras, quod est non videre—(3) sic et peccatum, quia non illustratur luce iustitiae, non intelligendo dinoscitur, sicuti tenebras dictum est non videndo sentiri. Et ad hoc pertinet, quod in psalmis dicitur: *Delicta quis intelligit?*

44. Quod autem ait: *Non enim quod volo, hoc ago, sed quod odi, illud facio. Si autem quod nolo, hoc facio, consentio legi, quoniam bona est,* satis quidem lex ab omni criminatione defenditur, sed cavendum, ne quis arbitretur his verbis auferri nobis liberum voluntatis arbitrium, quod non ita est. (2) Nunc enim homo describitur sub lege positus ante gratiam. Tunc enim peccatis vincitur, dum viribus suis iuste vivere conatur sine adiutorio liberantis gratiae dei. (3) In libero autem arbitrio habet, ut credat liberatori et accipiat gratiam, ut iam illo, qui eam donat, liberante et adiuvante non peccet atque ita desinat esse sub lege, sed cum lege vel in lege implens eam caritate dei, quod timore non poterat.

45-46. Quod autem ait: *Video aliam legem in membris meis repugnantem legi mentis meae et captivantem me sub lege peccati, quae est in membris meis,* legem peccati dicit, qua quisque carnali consuetudine implicatus adstringitur. (2) Hanc repugnare ait legi mentis suae et se captivare sub lege peccati, unde intelligitur ille homo describi, qui nondum est sub gratia. (3) Si enim repugnaret tantum consuetudo carnalis et non

without the law, it had lain hidden. (3) For each man, when he cannot fulfill a precept which he recognizes as just, acknowledges that he is dead. He sins all the more because of the criminal offense of the trespass than he would have without the prohibition. (4) Hence Paul concludes: "So that the sinner or the sin might be beyond measure because of the command" (7:13), for the offense was less prior to the Law, since where the Law is not, neither is there transgression.

41. "We know that the Law is spiritual, but I am carnal" (7:14), indicates clearly that the Law cannot be fulfilled except by spiritual men, who are made such by the grace of God. (2) For he who has become spiritual like the Law will easily fulfill what it prescribes; nor will he be under the Law, but with it. He is one, moreover, whom temporal goods do not seduce nor temporal evils terrify.

42. "I have been sold under sin" (7:14) means that everyone, by sinning, sells his own soul to the devil because he received as his price the sweetness of temporal pleasure. (2) Whence also the Lord has been called our Redeemer ["repurchaser"] because, as Paul has just said, we had been sold.

43. "I do not understand my own actions" (7:15) may seem to the less understanding to contradict Paul's earlier sentence, "Sin, to appear as sin, wrought death in me through what is good" (7:13). How can his sinfulness be made manifest if it is not understood? (2) "I do not understand" has the sense here of "I do not approve." For example, one does not see darkness, but discerns it in contrast to light: to perceive darkness is *not* to see it. (3) So also sin, because it is not illuminated by the light of righteousness, is discerned by not understanding, in the way that darkness is perceived by not seeing. Something in the Psalms pertains here: "Who understands his own transgressions?" (Ps. 18:13).

44. "For I do not want to do what I do; but what I hate, this I do. If, moreover, I do what I do not want to do, I agree that the Law is good" (7:15–16). Thus is the Law sufficiently defended from every accusation. But one must take care lest he think that these words deny our free will, for it is not so. (2) The man described here is under the Law, prior to grace; sin overcomes him when by his own strength he attempts to live righteously without the aid of God's liberating grace. (3) For by his free will man has a means to believe in the Liberator and to receive grace so that, with the liberating assistance of him who gives it, he might cease to sin. Thus might man cease to be under the Law, but rather be with or within it, fulfilling it by the love of God, which he could not do through fear.

45–46. "I see another law in my members warring against the law of my mind and making me captive to the law of sin which dwells in my members" (7:23). The law of sin holds everyone captive, entangled by carnal custom. (2) This law wars against the law of man's mind, capturing him under the law of sin, by which one understands that the man described here is not yet under grace. (3) If such carnal custom were merely to battle, yet not

captivaret, non esset damnatio. In eo enim est damnatio, quod obtemperamus et servimus desideriis pravis carnalibus. (4) Si autem existant et non desint talia desideria, non tamen his oboediamus, non captivamur et sub gratia iam sumus. De qua loquetur, cum exclamaverit et imploraverit liberatoris auxilium, ut possit per gratiam caritas, quod per legem timor non poterat. (5) Dixit enim: *Infelix ego homo; quis me liberabit de corpore mortis huius?* et subiecit: *Gratia dei per Iesum Christum dominum nostrum.* (6) Deinde incipit describere hominem sub gratia constitutum, qui tertius gradus est illorum quattuor, quos superius distinximus. Ad hunc gradum iam pertinet, quod statim subiungit: *Igitur ego ipse mente servio legi dei, carne autem legi peccati,* quia licet existentibus desideriis carnalibus iam non servit consentiendo ad faciendum peccatum, qui sub gratia constitutus mente servit legi dei, carne autem legi peccati. (7) Legem autem peccati dicit ex transgressione Adae conditionem mortalem, qua mortales facti sumus. Ex hac enim labe carnis concupiscentia carnalis sollicitat et secundum hanc dicit alio loco: *Fuimus et nos naturaliter filii irae sicut et ceteri.*

47. Quod autem dicit: *Nulla ergo condemnatio est nunc in his, qui sunt in Christo Iesu,* satis ostendit condemnationem non esse, si existant desideria carnalia, sed si eis ad peccandum oboediatur. (2) Quod contingit his, qui sub lege constituti sunt, nondum sub gratia. Nam sub lege constituti non solum repugnantem habent concupiscentiam, sed etiam captivi ducuntur, cum obtemperant ei. Non autem contingit his, qui mente serviunt legi dei.

48. Quod autem ait: *Quod enim impossibile erat legi, in quo infirmabatur per carnem: deus filium suum misit in similitudine carnis peccati et de peccato damnavit peccatum in carne, ut iustitia legis impleretur in nobis, qui non secundum carnem ambulamus sed secundum spiritum,* (2) manifestissime docet eadem ipsa praecepta legis propterea non impleta, quamvis essent implenda, quoniam, quibus data erat lex ante gratiam, dediti erant carnalibus bonis et ex his beatitudinem acquirere cupiebant neque metuebant, nisi cum talibus bonis imminebat adversitas, et ideo, cum illa bona temporalia turbarentur, facile recedebant a praeceptis legis. (3) Infirmabatur ergo lex non implendo, quod praecipiebat, non sua culpa sed per carnem, id est, per eos homines qui carnalia bona appetendo non amabant legis iustitiam sed ei temporalia commoda praeponebant. (4) Et ideo liberator noster dominus Iesus Christus suscipiendo mortalem carnem venit in similitudine carnis peccati. Carni enim peccati mors debita est. (5) At vero illa mors domini dignationis fuit, non debiti, et tamen hoc quoque apostolus peccatum vocat susceptionem mortalis carnis quamvis non peccatricis, ideo quia immortalis tamquam peccatum facit,

triumph, there would be no condemnation. Condemnation lies in the fact that we submit to and serve depraved carnal desires. (4) But if such desires abide constantly and yet we do not obey them, then we are not captured and we are now under grace. Paul will speak of grace when he calls upon and implores the aid of the Liberator, so that love through grace might accomplish what fear through the Law could not. (5) For he said, "Unhappy man that I am! Who will deliver me from this body of death?," and he answered, "The grace of God through Jesus Christ our Lord." (6) Here he begins to describe the man constituted under grace, the third of the four stages we distinguished above. What he immediately goes on to say pertains to this stage: "Therefore I myself serve the Law of God with my mind, but with my flesh I obey the law of sin" (7:25). Though his carnal desires still exist, by not consenting to sin he does not serve them who, constituted under grace, serves the law of God with his mind even though with his flesh he serves the law of sin. (7) Moreover, Paul calls the law of sin the mortal condition which has its source in the transgression of Adam, because of which we are born mortal. And from this falling-down of the flesh, concupiscence of the flesh troublingly entices us. About this concupiscence Paul says in another place, "We were by nature children of wrath, like the rest of mankind" (Eph. 2:3).

47. "For now there is no condemnation for those who are in Christ Jesus" (8:1). There is no condemnation if carnal desires exist, but only if one gives into them and sins. (2) And this is relevant to those constituted under the Law and not yet under grace, for not only does concupiscence fight against them: it captures them once they give into it. But this does not pertain to those who serve the Law of God with their minds.

48. "As to what was impossible for the Law, made weak by the flesh: God sent his own son in the likeness of the flesh of sin and by sin he condemned sin in the flesh, so that the righteousness of the Law might be fulfilled in us, who walk not according to the flesh but according to the Spirit" (8:3). (2) Here Paul most clearly teaches that these precepts of the Law were not fulfilled, though they ought to have been, because they who had the Law prior to grace were given over to fleshly goods and through these sought happiness. Nor did they fear except when adversity threatened these goods. So when these temporal goods were threatened, these people easily withdrew from the precepts of the Law. (3) Therefore the Law grew weaker as its prescriptions went unfulfilled—not through its own fault, but because of the flesh, that is, because these men who, seeking after fleshly goods, did not love the righteousness of the Law, but placed temporal comforts before it. (4) And so our Liberator the Lord Jesus Christ, by taking up mortal flesh, came in the likeness of the flesh of sin. For death is the wages of the flesh of sin. (5) But surely the Lord's death was an act of good will, not the payment of a debt. Yet nonetheless here too the Apostle calls Christ's assumption of mortal flesh "sin," even though he was without sin, because Christ, inasmuch as he is deathless, "made sin" (so to speak)

cum moritur. (6) Sed *de peccato,* inquit, *condemnavit peccatum in carne.* Id enim egit mors domini, ne mors timeretur et ex eo iam non appeterentur temporalia bona nec metuerentur temporalia mala, in quibus carnalis erat illa prudentia in qua impleri legis praecepta non
5 poterant. (7) Hac autem prudentia in homine dominico destructa et ablata iustitia legis impletur, cum secundum carnem non ambulatur, sed secundum spiritum. (8) Unde verissime dictum est: *Non veni legem solvere sed implere. Plenitudo ergo legis caritas.* Et caritas eorum est, qui secundum spiritum ambulant. (9) Haec enim ad gratiam pertinet spir-
10 itus sancti. Quando enim non erat caritas iustitiae sed timor, lex non implebatur.

49. Quod autem ait: *Quia prudentia carnis inimica in deum. Legi enim dei non est subiecta; nec enim potest,* ostendit, quid dixerit: *inimica,* ne quis putaret tamquam ex adverso principio aliquam naturam, quam non
15 condidit deus, inimicitias adversus deum exercere. (2) Inimicus ergo dei dicitur, qui legi ipsius non obtemperat et hoc per carnis prudentiam, id est, cum appetit temporalia bona et timet temporalia mala. (3) Definitio enim prudentiae in appetendis bonis et vitandis malis explicari solet. Quapropter recte appellat apostolus carnis prudentiam, qua haec
20 appetuntur pro magnis bonis, quae non perseverant cum homine, et ne haec amittantur timetur, quae quandoque amittenda sunt. (4) Non potest autem talis prudentia legi dei obtemperare, sed tunc obtemperatur legi, cum haec prudentia extincta fuerit, ut ei succedat prudentia spiritus, qua nec in bonis temporalibus spes nostra est neque in malis
25 timor. (5) Eadem namque animae natura et prudentiam carnis habet, cum inferiora sectatur, et prudentiam spiritus, cum superiora eligit, quemadmodum eadem aquae natura et frigore congelascit et calore resolvitur. (6) Sic ergo dictum est: *Legi dei non est subiecta prudentia carnis; neo enim potest,* quomodo recte diceretur nivem non posse
30 calefieri; neque enim potest, sed cum adhibito calore solvitur et calescit aqua, iam nemo potest eam nivem dicere.

50. Quod autem ait: *Corpus quidem mortuum est propter peccatum, spiritus autem vita est propter iustitiam,* corpus mortuum dicit mortale. (2) Ex ipsius enim mortalitate indigentia rerum terrenarum sollicitat
35 animam et quaedam desideria excitat, quibus ad peccandum non obtemperat, qui iam mente servit legi dei.

51. Quod autem ait: *Si spiritus eius, qui suscitavit Iesum Christum a mortuis, habitat in vobis, qui suscitavit Iesum Christum a mortuis, vivificabit et mortalia corpora vestra per inhabitantem spiritum eius in vobis,* iam
40 quartum gradum demonstrat ex illis quattuor, quos superius distinximus. (2) Sed gradus iste in hac vita non invenitur. Pertinet enim ad spem, qua exspectamus redemptionem corporis nostri, quando corruptibile hoc induet incorruptionem et mortale hoc induet immortalitatem. (3) Ibi pax perfecta est, quia nihil molestiarum anima de corpore pati-
45 tur iam vivificato et in caelestem qualitatem immutato.

when he died (cf. *Propp.* 32-34, 3; 2 Cor. 5:21). (6) But "by sin," Paul says, "he condemned sin in the flesh." For as a result of the Lord's death, those who had been wise in an earthly way, and so unable to fulfill the Law, ceased to fear death and neither sought worldly goods nor feared worldly evils. (7) Since the Lord as man has destroyed and removed this so-called wisdom, the righteousness of the Law is fulfilled when man does not walk according to the flesh, but to the spirit. (8) Whence it is most truly said, "I did not come to dissolve the Law but to fulfill it" (Mt 5:17). "For the fullness of the Law is love" (13:10), and love is theirs who walk according to the Spirit (9) whose grace pertains to this love. When therefore people feared rather than loved righteousness, the Law was not fulfilled.

49. "For the wisdom of the flesh is hostile to God; it is not subject to the Law of God, nor can it be" (8:7). Paul explains why he said "hostile," lest anyone think there is some nature born of an opposing principle that God did not create and that fights against God. (2) Paul states therefore that he who does not submit to God's Law is said to be hostile to God, and acts so because of the wisdom of the flesh, that is, in seeking worldly goods and fearing worldly evils. (3) For the usual definition of wisdom is to seek good and avoid evil. Wherefore rightly the Apostle names it the "wisdom of the flesh" when man seeks these lesser, transient goods and fears to lose what must be lost some day. (4) Nor, moreover, can such wisdom submit to the Law of God. But it will one day, when it is extinguished, superseded by the wisdom of the Spirit, on account of which we neither hope in temporal goods nor fear temporal evils. (5) For the soul has a single nature, and it has both the wisdom of the flesh when it follows inferior things, and the wisdom of the Spirit when choosing the superior, just as water's single nature both freezes from cold and melts from heat. (6) And so Paul said that "the wisdom of the flesh is not subject to the Law of God, nor can it be" in the same sense as one rightly says that snow cannot tolerate heat. For snow, once heated, melts and the *water* becomes warm, so that no one can then call it "snow."

50. "Indeed, the body is dead because of sin, but the spirit is life because of righteousness" (8:10). "The body is dead" means it is subject to death. (2) Because of this mortality the need for earthly things troubles the soul and arouses certain desires, to which he does not submit to the point of sinning who now serves the Law of God in his mind.

51. "If the spirit of him who raised Jesus Christ from the dead dwells in you, he who raised Jesus Christ from the dead will give life to your mortal bodies too, through his spirit dwelling in you" (8:11). Paul now points to the fourth of those four stages which we distinguished above. (2) But one does not reach this stage in this life; it pertains to that hope by which we await the redemption of our body, when this corruptible and mortal thing will put on incorruption and immortality (cf. 1 Cor. 15:53-4). (3) Then is there perfect peace, because the soul endures no troubles from the now-revivified body changed into a heavenly quality.

52. Quod autem ait: *Non enim accepistis spiritum servitutis in timorem, sed accepistis spiritum adoptionis filiorum, in quo clamamus abba, pater,* evidentissime duorum testamentorum distincta sunt tempora. Illud enim ad timorem pertinet, novum autem ad caritatem. (2) Sed quaeritur, quis sit spiritus servitutis? Nam spiritus adoptionis filiorum utique spiritus sanctus est, spiritus ergo servitutis in timore ille est, qui potestatem habet mortis, quia ipso timore per totam vitam rei erant servitutis, qui sub lege agebant, non sub gratia. (3) Nec mirandum est, quod eum acceperunt per divinam providentiam, qui bona temporalia sectabantur, non quia ipsius est lex et mandatum—(4) nam *lex sancta et mandatum sanctum et iustum et bonum,* ille autem spiritus servitutis non utique bonus, quem accipiunt qui praecepta datae legis implere non possunt, dum serviunt desideriis carnalibus nondum gratia liberatoris assumpti in filiorum adoptionem—sed quia et ipse spiritus servitutis non habet quemquam in potestate, nisi qui ei per ordinem divinae providentiae traditus fuerit dei iustitia sua cuique tribuente. (5) Quam potestatem acceperat apostolus, cum dicit de quibusdam: *Quos tradidi satanae, ut discant non blasphemare,* et iterum de alio: *Iam iudicavi,* inquit, *tradere huiusmodi satanae in interitum carnis, ut anima salva sit.* (6) Qui ergo nondum sub gratia sunt sed sub lege constituti vincuntur peccatis ad oboediendum desideriis carnalibus et praevaricatione augent reatum criminum suorum, spiritum acceperunt servitutis, id est spiritum eius, qui potestatem mortis habet. (7) Nam si spiritus servitutis ipsum spiritum hominis intellexerimus, incipit et spiritus adoptionis ipse intelligi tamquam in melius commutatus. (8) Sed quia spiritum adoptionis spiritum sanctum accipimus, quem manifeste ostendit, cum dicit: *Ipse spiritus testimonium reddit spiritui nostro,* (9) restat, ut spiritum servitutis illum intelligamus, cui serviunt peccatores, ut, quemadmodum spiritus sanctus a timore mortis vindicat, sic spiritus servitutis, qui potestatem habet mortis, eiusdem mortis terrore reos teneat, ut se ad liberatoris auxilium quisque convertat etiam ipso diabolo invito, qui eum semper in potestate habere desiderat.

53. Quod autem ait: *Nam expectatio creaturae revelationem filiorum dei expectat. Vanitati enim creatura subiecta est non sponte* et cetera usque ad id quod ait: *Et ipsi in nobismetipsis ingemiscimus adoptionem expectantes redemptionem corporis nostri,* (2) sic intelligendum est, ut neque sensum dolendi et gemendi opinemur esse in arboribus et oleribus et lapidibus et ceteris huiuscemodi creaturis—hic enim error Manichaeorum est—(3) neque angelos sanctos vanitati subiectos esse arbitremur et de his existimemus, quod liberabuntur a servitute interitus, cum interituri utique non sint, sed omnem creaturam in ipso homine sine ulla calumnia cogitemus. (4) Non enim creatura ulla esse potest nisi aut spiritualis,

52. "For you did not receive the spirit of slavery to cause fear, but you have received the spirit of the adoption of sons, by which we cry Abba, Father" (8:15). Most clearly Paul distinguishes between the periods of the two testaments, the one pertaining to fear, the new to love. (2) But, one asks, what is this spirit of slavery? Now since the spirit of adoption is surely the Holy Spirit, the spirit of slavery causing fear is therefore that one having the power of death. For on account of this fear, they who lived under the Law and not grace lived their whole lives under the spirit of slavery. (3) Nor is it surprising that they who pursued worldly goods received the spirit of slavery through divine providence, not because the Law and the commandment are of this spirit—(4) for "the Law is holy, and the commandment is holy, and just, and good" (7:12), and this spirit of slavery is by no means good. But they who cannot fulfill the precepts of the Law receive this spirit when they serve fleshly desires and are not yet taken up by the Liberator's grace into the adoption of sons—but because this spirit has no one in its power unless he be handed over by order of divine providence, for the righteousness of God gives each his due. (5) The Apostle had received such authority when he says about certain people "I have delivered them to Satan, that they might learn not to blaspheme" (1 Tim. 1:20), and again of someone else, "I have already decided to deliver this sort of man to Satan for the destruction of his body, so that his soul might be saved" (1 Cor. 5:3–5). (6) Therefore those who are not yet under grace but are constituted under the Law and beaten by sin into obeying fleshly desires, and increase the guilt of their crimes by transgression—these, I say, have received the spirit of slavery, that is, the spirit of him who has the power of death. (7) Now, if we were to take the 'spirit of slavery' to mean the spirit of man, then we would understand the 'spirit of adoption' as something like 'change for the better'. (8) But since by the 'spirit of adoption' we understand the Holy Spirit, to whom the Apostle obviously points when he says "The Spirit himself gives testimony to our spirit," (9) the spirit of slavery is then the one whom sinners serve. Just as the Holy Spirit frees one from death, so the Spirit of Slavery, who has the power of death, holds the guilty by fear of death. Thus each man turns himself to the aid of the Liberator even if the Devil himself, who wants to hold man forever in his power, fights against him.

53. "For the expectation of creation looks forward to the revelation of the sons of God. For creation was subject to futility, not of its own will" and so on up to where he says "and we ourselves groan inwardly awaiting adoption and the resurrection of our bodies" (8:19–23). (2) We should not think that this implies a sorrowing and sighing of trees and vegetables and stones and other suchlike creatures—for this is the error of the Manichees—(3) nor should we think that the holy angels are subject to futility, nor that they will be freed from the slavery of death, since they are entirely without death. Rather and without any false interpretation we take "every creature" to mean man himself. (4) For creatures range from the spiritual,

quae excellit in angelis, aut animalis quae etiam in vita bestiarum satis apparet, aut corporalis, quae videri aut tangi potest, omnis autem est etiam in homine, quia homo constat spiritu et anima et corpore. (5) Ergo *creatura revelationem filiorum dei expectat,* quicquid nunc in homine laborat et corruptioni subiacet, illam scilicet manifestationem, de qua idem dicit apostolus: (6) *Mortui enim estis et vita vestra abscondita est cum Christo in deo; cum Christus apparuerit vita vestra, tunc et vos apparebitis cum illo in gloria.* (7) Dicit et Iohannes: *Dilectissimi, nunc filii dei sumus et nondum apparuit, quid erimus; scimus autem, quia, cum apparuerit, similes ei erimus, quoniam videbimus eum sicuti est.* (8) Hanc ergo revelationem filiorum dei expectat creatura, quae in homine nunc vanitati subiecta est, quamdiu dedita est temporalibus rebus, quae transeunt tamquam umbra. (9) Unde et in psalmo dicitur: *Homo vanitati similis factus est, dies eius velut umbra praetereunt.* (10) De vanitate etiam Salomon loquitur, cum dicit: *Vanitas vanitantium et omnia vanitas, quae abundantia homini in omni labore suo, quo ipse laborat sub sole?* (11) De qua item David dicit: *Utquid diligitis vanitatem et quaeritis mendacium?* Non sponte autem dicit esse subiectam vanitati creaturam, quoniam poenalis est ista subiectio. (12) Non enim homo sicut sponte peccavit, sic etiam sponte damnatus est, quae tamen damnatio non sine spe reparationis irrogata est naturae nostrae. (13) Et ideo: *Propter eum,* inquit, *qui subiecit eam in spe, quia et ipsa creatura liberabitur a servitute interitus, in libertatem gloriae filiorum dei,* id est, etiam ipsa, quae tantummodo creatura est, nondum per fidem aggregata numero filiorum dei, sed tamen in eis, qui credituri erant, videbat apostolus, quod dicit, quia *creatura liberabitur a servitute interitus,* ut interitui non serviat, cui serviunt omnes peccatores. (14) Peccatori enim dictum est: *Morte morieris. Liberabitur* autem *in libertatem gloriae filiorum dei,* id est, ut et ipsa perveniat ad libertatem gloriae filiorum dei per fidem, quae fides cum in ea non erat tantummodo creatura dicebatur et ad ipsam refert, quod sequitur: *Scimus enim, quia creatura congemiscit et dolet usque adhuc.* (15) Erant enim adhuc credituri, qui etiam spiritu subiacebant laboriosis erroribus. Sed ne quis putaret de ipsorum tantum labore dictum esse, subiungit etiam de his, qui iam crediderant. (16) Quamquam enim spiritu, hoc est, mente servirent legi dei, tamen quia carne servitur legi peccati, quamdiu molestias et sollicitationes mortalitatis nostrae patimur, ideo addidit dicens: (17) *Non solum autem sed et nos ipsi primitias spiritus habentes et ipsi in nobismetipsis ingemiscimus.* (18) Non solum ergo inquit ipsa, quae tantummodo creatura dicitur in hominibus, qui nondum crediderunt et ideo nondum in filiorum dei numero constituti sunt, congemiscit et dolet, sed etiam nosmetipsi, qui

whose ultimate expression is the angels, to the animal, expressed in the life of beasts, to the corporeal, which can be seen and touched. But all these aspects unite in man who exists as spirit, soul, and body. (5) Therefore "creation awaits the revelation of the sons of God," especially whatever now labors in man and is subject to corruption. This is precisely that manifestation of which the same Apostle says: (6) "For you have died and your life has been hidden with Christ in God; when Christ who is your life will have appeared, then you also will appear with him in glory" (Col. 3:3-4). (7) And John says: "Most beloved, now we are sons of God. It has not yet appeared what we shall be, but we know that when he appears, we will be like him, for we shall see him as he is" (1 Jn. 3:2). (8) And so creation awaits this revelation of the sons of God, that now in man remains subject to futility as long as it is given over to temporal things, which pass like a shadow. (9) Whence also the psalm says: "Man has been made like to vanity; his days pass like a shadow" (Ps. 143:4). (10) Solomon too speaks of vanity when he says: "Vanity of the vain, all is vanity. What profit does a man have by all his labor, on account of which he labors under the sun?"[2] (Eccle. 1:2-3). (11) And David says: "Why do you love vanity and seek falsehood?" (Ps. 4:3). Moreover, Paul says that creation was not subjected to vanity willingly, since this subjection is penal. (12) For though man sinned willingly he did not willingly receive condemnation, though this condemnation was inflicted on our natures not without hope of restoration. (13) And so Paul says: "Because of him who subjected it in hope, even creation which itself will be set free from its slavery to death into the glorious liberty of the sons of God" (8:21). That is, the Apostle saw that this mere creature who was not yet joined through faith to the number of the sons of God would nonetheless eventually number among those who would believe. And so he said, "creation will be freed from its bondage to decay" so that it will not serve death, which all sinners serve. (14) For it was said to the sinner: "By death will you die" (Gen. 2:17). But creation "will be set free into the glorious liberty of the sons of God," that is, even creation, which was called only "creation" since faith was not yet in it, might itself attain the glorious liberty of the sons of God through faith. What follows refers to this: "For we know that creation sighs and sorrows up til now." (15) For some who were about to believe still continued spiritually in distressing errors. But lest anyone think that Paul spoke only of their difficulty, he now speaks concerning those who already believed. (16) For although with the spirit—that is, with the mind—they served the Law of God, nonetheless the flesh serves the law of sin as long as we endure our mortal vexations and anxieties. Thus, Paul continues, (17) "Not only creation but we ourselves who have the first fruits of the Spirit groan inwardly" (8:23). (18) In other words, not only does that creaturely part of those not yet faithful, and hence not yet among the sons of God, groan and sorrow, but also we who

---

2. *Vanitas vanitantium.* Augustine's text is faulty. Cf. *Retr.* I. 7,3

credimus et spiritus primitias habemus, quia iam spiritu adhaeremus
deo per fidem et ideo non iam creatura sed filii dei appellamur, (19)
tamen et *ipsi in nobismetipsis ingemiscimus adoptionem expectantes redemptionem corporis nostri.* (20) Haec enim adoptio, quae iam facta est in his
5 qui crediderunt spiritu non corpore facta est. Nondum enim etiam
corpus reformatum est in caelestem illam immutationem, sicut spiritus
iam mutatus est reconciliatione fidei ab erroribus conversus ad deum.
(21) Ergo etiam in his, qui crediderunt, expectatur adhuc illa manifestatio, quae in corporis resurrectione proveniet, quae pertinet ad quar-
10 tum illum gradum, ubi ex toto perfecta pax erit et quies aeterna nulla
nobis ex aliqua parte corruptione resistente aut sollicitante molestia.

54. Quod autem ait: *Similiter et spiritus adiuvat infirmitatem nostram; quid enim oremus, sicut oportet, nescimus,* manifestum est eum de spiritu sancto dicere, quod in consequentibus clarum est, ubi ait: (2) *Quia
15 secundum deum interpellat pro sanctis.* Nos ergo *quid oremus, sicut oportet, nescimus* duas ob res, quod et illud, quod futurum speramus et quo tendimus, nondum apparet et in hac ipsa vita multa possunt nobis prospera videri, quae adversa sunt, et adversa quae prospera. (3) Nam et tribulatio quando accidit servo dei ad probationem vel emendationem,
20 videtur nonnumquam minus intelligentibus inutilis, sed si referatur ad illud quod dictum est: (4) *Da nobis auxilium de tribulatione et vana salus hominis,* intelligitur quia plerumque de tribulatione nos adiuvat deus, et frustra salus optatur, quae aliquando adversa est, cum delectatione et amore huius vitae implicat animam. (5) Inde est etiam illud: *Tribula-
25 tionem et dolorem inveni et nomen domini invocavi.* Cum enim dicit: *inveni,* significat utilem. Non enim recte gratulamur nos invenisse, nisi quod quaerebamus. (6) Ergo *quid oremus, sicut oportet, nescimus.* Deus enim novit et quid nobis in hac vita expediat et quid post hanc vitam daturus sit. (7) Sed *ipse spiritus interpellat gemitibus inenarrabilibus.*
30 Gemere dicit spiritum, quod nos gemere faciat caritate concitans desiderium futurae vitae, sicut dicit: *Temptat vos dominus deus vester, ut sciat, si diligitis eum,* id est, ut scire vos faciat. Non enim deum aliquid latet.

55. Quod autem ait: *Quos vocavit, ipsos et iustificavit,* potest movere
35 et quaeri utrum omnes qui vocati sunt, iustificentur. Sed alibi legimus: *Multi vocati, pauci autem electi.* (2) Tamen quia ipsi quoque electi utique vocati sunt, manifestum est non iustificatos nisi vocatos quamquam non omnes vocatos sed eos, *qui secundum propositum vocati sunt,* sicut superius dicit. (3) Propositum autem dei accipiendum est, non
40 ipsorum. Ipse autem exponit, quid sit secundum propositum, cum dicit: *Quoniam quos ante praescivit, et praedestinavit conformes imaginis filii eius.* (4) Non enim omnes, qui vocati sunt, secundum propositum vocati sunt. Hoc enim propositum ad praescientiam et ad praedestinationem dei pertinet.

believe and have the first fruits of the spirit, since we now cling by our spirit to God through faith and hence are called not 'creation' but 'sons of God', (19) even we "groan inwardly as we await adoption, the redemption of our bodies" (8:23). (20) For this adoption, already established for those who have believed, was accomplished only spiritually, not physically. For the body has not yet been remade by that heavenly transformation, as the spirit has already been changed through the reconciliation of faith, having turned from its errors to God. (21) Therefore, even those who believe still await that manifestation to come at the resurrection of the body. This is that fourth stage of complete and perfect peace and eternal rest, utterly free of contending corruption and anxious vexation.

54. "Similarly also the Spirit helps our weakness, for we do not know what to pray for as we ought" (8:26). Paul speaks here of the Holy Spirit, as is clear from what follows: (2) "since according to the will of God the Spirit intercedes for the saints." We "do not know what to pray for as we ought" for two reasons. First, the future goal of our hopes and efforts remains unclear and, second, in this life many things to us can seem favorable that are in fact unfavorable, and vice versa. (3) For tribulation, when it befalls a servant of God to test or correct him, seems sometimes futile to those with less understanding. But if one recalls (4) "Grant to us the aid of tribulation, for the well-being of man is hollow" (Ps. 59:13), he understands that God often helps us by tribulation; and well-being, which is sometimes unfavorable, is wrongly longed for when it entangles the soul with delight and love of this life. (5) Whence likewise: "I came upon tribulation and sorrow, and I invoked the name of the Lord" (Ps. 114:3-4). For in saying "came upon," he means that tribulation is useful, for we do not rightly rejoice in coming upon something unless we were seeking it. (6) And therefore "we do not know what to pray for as we ought," for God knows what is advantageous for us in this life and what he will give us after this life. (7) But "the Spirit itself intercedes with inexpressible groans" (8:26). He says that the Spirit groans insofar as it makes us groan, rousing in us by love the desire for the future life, as it says: "The Lord your God tempts you, so that he might know if you love him" (Deut. 13:3), that is, in order to make *you* know, for nothing is hidden from God.

55. "Those whom he called, these also he justified" (8:30) can likewise lead to the question whether all who are called are justified. But elsewhere we read, "Many are called, but few are chosen" (Mt 22:14). (2) Still, since the elect have certainly been called, they obviously are not justified unless they have been called. But not all are called to justification, only those who are "called according to the purpose," as Paul said above (8:28). (3) This purpose, it must be understood, is God's, not theirs who are called. Paul explains "according to the purpose" when he says: "Since those whom he foreknew he also predestined to be conformed to the image of his son" (8:29). (4) For not all who are called are called according to the purpose, for that purpose pertains to the foreknowledge and predestination of God.

Nec praedestinavit aliquem, nisi quem praescivit crediturum et secuturum vocationem suam, quos et electos dicit. (5) Multi enim non veniunt, cum vocati fuerint, nemo autem venit, qui vocatus non fuerit.

56. Quod autem dicit: *Ut sit primogenitus in multis fratribus,* satis docet aliter intelligendum dominum nostrum unigenitum aliter primogenitum. (2) Nam ubi unigenitus dicitur, fratres non habet et naturaliter est filius dei, verbum in principio, per quod facta sunt omnia. (3) Secundum susceptionem autem hominis et incarnationis dispensationem, per quam nos etiam non naturaliter filios in adoptionem filiorum vocare dignatus est, primogenitus dictur cum adiunctione fratrum. (4) Ubi enim primus dicitur, non utique solus sed consecuturis fratribus in quo ipse praecessit. Unde et alio loco primogenitum eum a mortuis dicit, ut sit in omnibus ipse primatum tenens. (5) Resurrectio enim mortuorum, ut iam non moriantur, ante illum nulla, post illum autem multorum sanctorum est, quos fratres non confunditur appellare propter ipsam communicationem humanitatis.

57. Quod autem dicit: *Quis nos separabit a caritate Christi? tribulatio an angustia an persecutio?* et cetera, ex superiore sententia pendet, ubi ait: (2) *Si tamen compatimur, ut et glorificemur. Existimo enim, quod non sint condignae passiones huius temporis ad futuram gloriam, quae revelabitur in nobis.* (3) Ad ipsam enim hortationem omnis huius loci intentio directa est, ne illi, quibus loquitur, persecutionibus frangerentur, si viverent secundum prudentiam carnis, qua temporalia bona appentuntur et timentur temporalia mala.

58. Quod autem dicit: *Certus sum enim* et non dixit: opinor enim, plena fide tenuit, *quod nec mors* ulla *nec vita* temporalis promissa nec cetera subsequentia possunt credentem a caritate dei detorquere. (2) Nemo ergo separat: nec qui minatur mortem, quia, qui credit in Christo, licet moriatur, vivet; neque qui pollicetur vitam, quia ille dat vitam aeternam. (3) Nam temporalis vitae pollicitatio aeternae comparatione contemnenda est. *Neque angelus* separat, quia *licet angelus,* inquit, *de caelo descendat et annuntiet vobis, praeterquam quod accepistis, anathema sit.* (4) *Neque principatus,* id est contrarius, quia exuit se ipse hos principatus et potestates triumphans eos in semetipso. (5) *Neque praesentia neque futura,* id est temporalia, vel quae delectant vel quae premunt vel quae spem dant vel quae incutiunt timorem. *Neque virtus*—(6) et hic virtutem contrariam oportet intelligi, secundum quam dicit: *Nemo vasa fortis diripiet, nisi prius alligaverit forte. Neque altitudo neque profundum.* (7)Plerumque enim inanis curiositas earum rerum, quae inveniri non possunt aut frustra etiam inveniuntur sive in caelo sive in abysso, separat a deo, nisi caritas vincat, quae ad certa spiritualia non

Nor did God predestine anyone except him whom he knew would believe and would follow the call. Paul designates such persons "the elect." (5) For many do not come, though they have been called; but no one comes who has not been called.

56. "In order that he might be the first-born of many brothers" (8:29). Paul makes it sufficiently clear that we should understand our Lord as "only-begotten" in one way, and as "first-born" in another. (2) For where he is called "only-begotten," he has no brethren, and is by nature the Son of God, the Word in the beginning through whom all things were made. (3) However, by his assumption of humanity and the dispensation of the Incarnation, through which even we who are not naturally sons may be called into the adoption of sons, he is said to be the "first-born," and has brothers. (4) For "first" indicates that he is not alone, but leads his brothers who follow where he preceded. Whence also Paul elsewhere calls him the first-born from the dead, so that in all things he might be preeminent (Col. 1:18). (5) For before him there was no resurrection of the dead that men might die no more; but now after him come many saints, whom he does not hesitate to call "brothers," because he shares in their humanity.

57. "Who will separate us from the love of Christ? Will tribulation or anxiety or persecution?" (8:35) etc., depends on the earlier sentence, (2) "If we suffer in order that we might be glorified, I consider the sufferings of the present time not worth comparing to the future glory that is to be revealed to us" (8:17-18). (3) Paul means by this to exhort his listeners not to be broken by persecution, in case they had been living according to the wisdom of the flesh, and so desiring worldly goods and fearing worldly ills.

58. Moreover, Paul says "I am certain," and not "I am of the opinion." He thus shows his total faith that neither death nor promised temporal life nor any other thing he enumerates can tear the believer from the love of God. (2) Therefore no one separates the believer from God: neither he who threatens death, for he who believes in Christ, though he die, will live; nor he who promises life, because Christ gives life eternal. (3) For the promise of temporal life must be despised when compared to the promise of eternal life. Nor can an angel separate us, because "even if an angel were to come down from heaven and announce to you something other than what you have received, let him be anathema" (Gal. 1:8). (4) Nor can a "principality," that is, an opposing power, since Christ himself has cast aside these principalities and powers, vanquishing them in himself (cf. Col. 2:15). (5) "Nor things present nor things to come," that is, temporal things, whether those that delight or oppress or give hope or instill fear. "Nor power"—(6) and here it is right to understand "power" as "opposing power," as Christ says: "No one can carry away the goods of a strong man unless he has first bound the strong man" (Mt 12:29). "Nor height nor depth," (7) for often empty curiosity about things which are either unknowable or known in vain, whether in heaven or in the depths, separates one from God, unless love triumphs. For love summons men to sure spiritual knowledge, not by the

vanitate rerum, quae foris sunt, sed interno lumine invitat. (8) *Neque creatura alia,* quod duobus modis intelligi potest: aut visibilis creatura, quia et nos id est anima creatura sumus, sed invisibilis, ut hoc dixerit, quod nos non separat alia creatura, id est amor corporum; aut certe
5 quia nos non separat alia creatura a caritate dei, ex eo quod nulla creatura est alia inter nos et deum, quae se opponat et a complexu eius excludat. (9) Supra humanas enim mentes quae rationales sunt, iam nulla creatura sed deus est.

59. Quod autem dicit: *Quorum patres, ex quibus Christus secundum*
10 *carnem,* et adiecit: *Qui est super omnes deus benedictus in saecula,* plenissimam fidem commendat, quia dominum nostrum et secundum susceptionem carnis filium hominis confitemur, et secundum aeternitatem verbum in principio deum benedictum super omnes in saecula. (2) Huius autem confessionis Iudaei quoniam partem tenuerunt, refellun-
15 tur a domino. Nam cum eos interrogasset, cuius filium dicerent esse Christum, responderunt David. (3) Hoc autem secundum carnem est. De divinitate vero eius, quod deus est, nihil responderunt. Ideo dominus ait eis: *Quomodo ergo David in spiritu vocat eum dominum?* (4) ut intelligerent hoc se confessos esse tantum, quod Christus filius est
20 David, hoc autem tacuisse quod est Christus dominus ipsius David. (5) Illud enim est secundum susceptionem carnis, hoc secundum aeternitatem divinitatis.

60. Quod autem ait: *Nondum enim nascentium neque agentium aliquid boni aut mali, ut secundum electionem propositum dei maneret, non ex*
25 *operibus sed ex vocante, dictum est ei: Quia maior serviet minori, sicut scriptum est: Iacob dilexi, Esau autem odio habui,* (2) nonnullos movet, ut putent apostolum Paulum abstulisse liberum voluntatis arbitrium, quo promeremur deum bono pietatis vel malo impietatis offendimus. (3) Dicunt enim, quod ante opera aliqua seu bona seu mala duorum non-
30 dum nascentium deus unum dilexerit, alterum odio habuerit. (4) Sed respondemus praescientia dei factum esse, qua novit etiam de nondum natis, qualis quisque futurus sit. Sed ne quis dicat: Opera ergo elegit deus in eo, quem dilexit, quamquam nondum erant, quod ea futura praesciebat; quod si opera elegit, quomodo dicit apostolus non ex
35 operibus factam electionem? (5) Propterea ergo intelligendum est opera bona per dilectionem fieri, dilectionem autem esse in nobis per donum spiritus sancti, sicut idem dicit apostolus: (6) *Caritas dei diffusa est in cordibus nostris per spiritum sanctum, qui datus est nobis.* Non ergo quisquam gloriari debet ex operibus tamquam suis, quae per donum dei
40 habet, cum ipsa dilectio in eo bonum operatur. (7) Quid ergo elegit deus? Si enim cui vult, donat spiritum sanctum, per quem dilectio bonum operatur, quomodo elegit, cui donet? (8) Si enim

vanity of exterior things, but by inner light. (8) "Nor any other creature." This can be understood in two ways. First, as a visible creature (since we too—that is, we as "soul"—are "creature," but invisible). By this interpretation Paul would mean that no other creature, that is, the love of [visible] bodies, separates us. Or, surely, this could also mean that no other creature can separate us from the love of God because no other creature stands between us and God, opposing us and keeping us from God's embrace. (9) For above human minds, which are rational, there is no other creature, only God.

59. "To them belong the patriarchs and of their race according to the flesh is Christ," and he added, "who is God over all, blessed forever" (9:5). The Apostle commends a most full faith, since we confess our Lord to be both the Son of Man according to his taking up the flesh, and according to eternity, the Word in the Beginning, God blessed over all forever. (2) The Lord refutes those Jews who held only the first part of this confession. For when he had asked them whose son they said the Christ was, they answered "David's" (Mt 22:42-3). (3) This is so according to the flesh. But concerning his divinity, the fact that he is God, they answered nothing. And so the Lord said to them, "Why did David, inspired, call him 'Lord'?" (Mt 22:43), (4) so that they might understand that they had only confessed Christ as the son of David, but had been silent on the point that Christ is the Lord of this same David. (5) The one fact follows from the assumption of the flesh, the other from the eternity of divinity.

60. "For when they were not yet born, nor had they done anything either good or evil, in order that the purpose of God's election might continue, not because of works but because of his call, she was told, 'the elder will serve the younger', as it is written, 'Jacob I loved, but Esau I hated'" (9:11-13). (2) This moves some people to think that the apostle Paul had done away with the freedom of the will, by which we earn the esteem of God by the good of piety, or offend him by the evil of impiety. (3) For, these people say, God loved the one and hated the other before either was even born and could have done either good or evil. (4) But we answer that God did this by his foreknowledge, by which he knows the character even of the unborn. But no one should say, "Therefore God chose the works of the man he loved, although these works did not exist, because he foreknew what they would be." If God elected works, why does the Apostle say that election is not according to works? (5) For this very reason, then, one should understand that we are able to do good works through love, and we have love through the gift of the Holy Spirit, as the Apostle himself says: (6) "For the love of God has been poured into our hearts by the Holy Spirit, which has been given to us" (5:5). Therefore no one should glory in his works as though they were his own, for he does them by the gift of God, since this love itself works good in him. (7) What then has God elected? For if he gives the Holy Spirit, through whom love works good, to whomever he wishes, how does he choose the Spirit's recipient? (8) If he

nullo merito, non est electio. Aequales enim omnes sunt ante meritum nec potest in rebus omnino aequalibus electio nominari. (9) Sed quoniam spiritus sanctus non datur nisi credentibus, non quidem deus elegit opera, quae ipse largitur, cum dat spiritum sanctum, ut per carita-
5 tem bona operemur, sed tamen elegit fidem. (10) Quia nisi quisque credat in eum et in accipiendi voluntate permaneat, non accipit donum dei, id est spiritum sanctum, per quem diffusa caritate bonum possit operari. (11) Non ergo elegit deus opera cuiusquam in praescientia, quae ipse daturus est, sed fidem elegit in praescientia, ut quem sibi
10 crediturum esse praescivit ipsum elegerit, cui spiritum sanctum daret, ut bona operando etiam aeternam vitam consequeretur. (12) Dicit enim idem apostolus: *Idem deus, qui operatur omnia in omnibus,* nusquam autem dictum est: deus credit omnia in omnibus. Quod ergo credimus, nostrum est, quod autem bonum operamur, illius qui
15 credentibus in se dat spiritum sanctum. (13) Hoc autem exemplum quibusdam Iudaeis obiectum est, qui Christo crediderant et de operibus ante gratiam gloriabantur et dicebant se ipsam evangelii gratiam per sua bona opera praecedentia meruisse, cum bona opera in nullo esse possint, nisi qui acceperit gratiam. (14) Est autem gratia, ut vocatio pecca-
20 tori praerogetur, cum eius merita nulla, nisi ad damnationem praecesserint. (15) Quod si vocatus vocantem secutus fuerit, quod est iam in libero arbitrio, merebitur et spiritum sanctum per quem bona possit operari, in quo permanens—quod nihilominus est in libero arbitrio—merebitur etiam vitam aeternam, quae nulla possit labe cor-
25 rumpi.

61. Quod autem ait: *Miserebor, cui misertus ero, et misericordiam praestabo, cui misericors fuero,* hinc ostenditur non esse iniquitatem apud deum, quod possunt dicere quidam cum audiunt: *Antequam nascerentur Iacob dilexi, Esau autem odio habui.* (2) *Miserebor enim,* inquit,
30 *cui misertus ero.* Primo enim misertus est nostri deus, cum peccatores essemus, ut vocaret nos. (3) *Cui ergo misertus ero,* inquit, ut eum vocem, *miserebor* adhuc eius, cum crediderit. Quomodo autem adhuc, nisi ut credenti et petenti det spiritum sanctum? (4) Quo dato misericordiam praestabit, cui misericors fuerit, id est, ut faciat eum misericor-
35 dem, quo bona possit per dilectionem operari. (5) Nemo ergo sibi audeat tribuere, quod misericorditer operatur, quia deus illi per spiritum sanctum dedit dilectionem, sine qua nemo potest esse misericors. (6) Non ergo elegit deus bene operantes sed credentes potius, ut ipse illos faciat bene operari. (7) Nostrum enim est credere et velle, illius
40 autem dare credentibus et volentibus facultatem bene operandi per

does not choose according to merit, it is not election, for all are equal prior to merit, and no choice can be made between absolutely equal things. (9) But since he gives the Holy Spirit only to believers, God indeed does not choose works, which he himself bestows, for he gives the Spirit freely so that through love we might do good, but rather he chooses faith. (10) For unless each one believes in him and perseveres in his willingness to receive, he does not receive the gift of God, that is, the Holy Spirit, whose pouring forth of love enables him to do good. (11) Therefore God did not elect anyone's works (which God himself will grant) by foreknowledge, but rather by foreknowledge he chose faith, so that he chooses precisely him whom he foreknew would believe in him; and to him he gives the Holy Spirit, so that by doing good works he will as well attain eternal life. (12) For the same Apostle says: "It is the same God who *works* all things in all" (1 Cor. 12:6). Nowhere is it said, "God *believes* all things to all" (cf. 1 Cor. 13:7). Belief is our work, but good deeds are his who gives the Holy Spirit to believers. (13) This argument was used against certain Jews who, once they believed in Christ, both gloried in the works they did before receiving grace and claimed that they had merited this same grace of the Gospel by their own previous good works, though only the person who has already received grace can do good works. (14) Moreover, the nature of grace is such that the call precedes merit, reaching the sinner when he had deserved only damnation. (15) But if he follows God's call of his own free will, he will merit also the Holy Spirit, through whom he can do good works. And remaining in the Spirit—no less also by free will—he will also merit life eternal, which cannot be marred by any flaw.

61. "I will have mercy on whom I will have had mercy, and I will show him compassion on whom I will have had compassion" (9:11–15).[3] Here Paul shows that there is no iniquity with God, as certain people can say when they hear "Before they were born, Jacob I loved, but Esau I hated." (2) "I will have mercy," he says, "on whom I will have had mercy." God was merciful to us the first time when he called us while we were still sinners. (3) "On whom I will have had mercy," he says, "so that I called him," and *still* "I will have mercy on him" yet again once the man has believed. Yet how does God have mercy this second time? He gives to the believing seeker the Holy Spirit. (4) Now, having given the Spirit, God will then give compassion to those to whom he has already been compassionate. That is, he will make the believer compassionate, so that he can do good works through love. (5) Hence let no one dare to credit himself when he acts compassionately, since God gave him this love through the Holy Spirit, without which no one can be compassionate. (6) Therefore God did not elect those doing good works, but those who believed, with the result that he enabled them to do good works. (7) It is we who believe and will, but he who gives to those believing and willing the ability to do good works

---

3. Augustine's exegesis demands strict attention to Latin sequence of tenses.

spiritum sanctum, per quem caritas dei diffunditur in cordibus nostris, ut nos misericordes efficiat.

62. Quod autem ait: *Igitur non volentis neque currentis, sed miserentis est dei,* non tollit liberum voluntatis arbitrium, sed non sufficere dicit velle nostrum, nisi adiuvet deus misericordes nos efficiendo ad bene operandum per donum spiritus sancti—ad hoc referens, quod superius dixit: (2) *Miserebor, cui misertus ero, et misericordiam praestabo, cui misericors fuero*—(3) quia neque velle possumus nisi vocemur, et cum post vocationem voluerimus, non sufficit voluntas nostra et cursus noster, nisi deus et vires currentibus praebeat et perducat quo vocat. (4) Manifestum est ergo non volentis neque currentis, sed miserentis dei esse, quod bene operamur, quamquam ibi sit etiam voluntas nostra, quae sola nihil posset. (5) Unde sequitur etiam de Pharaonis supplicio testimonium, cum ait scriptura de Pharaone: *Quia ad hoc te excitavi, ut ostendam in te potentiam meam et ut annuntietur nomen meum in universa terra.* Sicut enim legimus in Exodo, (6) obduratum est cor Pharaonis ut tam evidentibus signis non moveretur. Quod ergo tunc Pharao non obtemperabat praeceptis dei, iam de supplicio veniebat. (7) Non autem quisquam potest dicere obdurationem illam cordis immerito accidisse Pharaoni, sed iudicio dei retribuentis incredulitati eius debitam poenam. (8) Non ergo hoc illi imputatur, quod tunc non obtemperaret, quandoquidem obdurato corde obtemperare non poterat, sed quia dignum se praebuit, cui cor obduraretur, priore infidelitate. (9) Sicut enim in his, quos elegit deus, non opera sed fides inchoat meritum, ut per munus dei bene operentur, sic in his quos damnat, infidelitas et impietas inchoat poenae meritum, ut per ipsam poenam etiam male operentur, sicut et superius idem dicit apostolus: (10) *Et quoniam non probaverunt deum in notitia habere, tradidit illos deus in reprobum sensum, ut faciant quae non conveniunt.* (11) Quapropter ita concludit apostolus: *Ergo cuius vult miseretur et quem vult obdurat.* (12) Cuius enim miseretur, facit eum bene operari et, quem obdurat, relinquit eum, ut male operetur. Sed et illa misericordia praecedenti merito fidei tribuitur et ista obduratio praecedenti impietati, (13) ut et bona per donum dei operemur et mala per supplicium, cum tamen homini non auferatur liberum voluntatis arbitrium sive ad credendum deo, ut consequatur nos misericordia, sive ad impietatem, ut consequatur supplicium. (14) Qua conclusione illata infert quaestionem tamquam a contradicente. Ait enim: *Dicis itaque mihi: Quid adhuc conqueritur? Nam voluntati eius quis resistit?* (15) Cui sane inquisitioni sic respondet, ut intelligamus spiritualibus viris et iam non secundum terrenum hominem viventibus patere posse prima merita fidei et impietatis, quomodo deus praescius eligat credituros et damnet incredulos, (16) nec ex operibus illos eligens nec istos ex operibus damnans, sed illorum fidei praestans, ut bene operentur, et istorum impietatem obdurans deserendo, ut male operentur. (17) Qui quoniam intellectus

through the Holy Spirit, through which the love of God is poured forth in our hearts, thus making us compassionate.

62. "Therefore it depends not on man's willing or running, but on God's mercy" (9:15). Paul does not take away the freedom of the will, but says our will does not suffice unless God helps us, making us merciful so that we can do good works through the gift of the Holy Spirit, as he had just said above, (2) "I will have mercy on whom I will have had mercy, and I will show him compassion on whom I will have had compassion." (3) For neither can we will unless we are called, nor after our calling, once we have willed, is our will and our running sufficient unless God both gives strength to our running and leads where he calls. (4) Therefore, clearly, we do good deeds not by our own willing or running but by the mercy of God, although our will (which alone can do nothing) is also present. (5) And this relates to Pharaoh's punishment, where Scripture says: "I have raised you up for this purpose, to show my power in you, so that my name might be proclaimed in all the earth" (9:17). And thus we read in Exodus that (6) Pharaoh's heart was hardened, so that he remained unmoved even by clear signs (cf. Ex. 10:1). Thus Pharaoh's disobedience to God's commands came as a punishment. (7) And no one can say that this hardness of heart befell Pharaoh undeservedly: it was the penalty of the just judgment of God punishing his unbelief. (8) Nor should one think that Pharaoh did not obey because he could not because his heart had been hardened. Rather, he had merited his hardness of heart by his prior infidelity. (9) For as with the chosen (not works but faith initiating merit so that through the gift of God they do good), so with the condemned: infidelity and impiety initiate their meriting their penalty. Thus because of the punishment itself they do evil, as the same Apostle says above: (10) "And since they did not see fit to acknowledge God, God handed them over to a base mind so that they did unseemly things" (1:28). (11) Wherefore the Apostle concludes: "Therefore he has mercy on whom he will and hardens whom he will" (9:18). (12) On whom he has mercy, he causes him to do good, and whom he hardens, he leaves to doing evil. But that mercy was given to the preceding merit of faith, and that hardening to preceding impiety, (13) so that we work both good deeds through the gift of God and evil through his chastisement. Nevertheless, man's free will remains, whether for belief in God so that mercy follows, or for impiety followed by punishment. (14) Having delivered this conclusion, Paul introduces a question as if from an opponent: "You say to me, 'Why does he even now find fault? For who resists his will?'" (9:19). (15) He responds to this question sensibly, so that we might understand that only to spiritual and not to earthly men are these difficult issues made clear, issues like the first merits of faith and impiety, the way God in his foreknowledge elects those who will believe and condemns the unbelieving, (16) neither electing nor condemning because of works, but granting to the faith of the one group the ability to do good works, and hardening the impiety of the other by deserting them, so that they do evil. (17) This understanding, as I have said, is given only to spiri-

ut dixi spiritualibus patet, a carnali autem prudentia longe remotus est, sic refellit inquirentem, ut intelligat se deponere debere prius hominem luti, ut ista per spiritum investigare mereatur. (18) Itaque inquit: *O homo, tu quis es, qui respondeas deo? Numquid dicit figmentum ei, qui se finxit: Quare sic me fecisti? Annon habet potestatem figulus luti ex eadem conspersione vas facere, aliud quidem in honorem, aliud in contumeliam?* (19) Quamdiu figmentum es, inquit, et ad massam luti pertines nondum perductus ad spiritualia, ut sis spiritualis omnia iudicans et a nemine iudiceris, cohibeas te oportet ab huiusmodi inquisitione et non respondeas deo. (20) Cuius consilium quisque scire cupiens oportet, ut prius in eius amicitiam recipiatur, quod contingere nisi spiritualibus non potest iam portantibus imaginem caelestis hominis. *Iam, enim inquit, non vos dicam servos sed amicos. Omnia enim, quae audivi a patre meo, nota feci vobis.* (21) Quamdiu itaque vas figuli est, conterendum est hoc ipsum in te prius virga illa ferrea, de qua dictum est: (22) *Reges eos in virga ferrea et tamquam vas figuli conteres eos,* ut corrupto exteriore homine et interiore renovato possis in caritate radicatus et fundatus comprehendere longitudinem, latitudinem, altitudinem et profundum, cognoscere etiam supereminentem scientiam caritatis dei. (23) Nunc itaque cum ex eadem conspersione deus alia vasa in honorem fecit, alia in contumeliam, non est tuum discutere, quisquis secundum hanc conspersionem adhuc vivis, id est, terreno sensu et carnaliter sapis.

63. Quod autem ait: *Attulit in multa patientia vasa irae, quae perfecta sunt in perditionem,* hinc satis significavit obdurationem illam cordis, quae in Pharaone facta est, ex meritis venisse occultae superioris impietatis, (2) quam tamen patienter sustinuit deus, donec ad illud tempus perduceretur, quo opportune in eum vindicta procederet, ad correctionem eorum, quos ab errore instituerat liberare et ad cultum suum pietatemque revocando perducere precibus eorum et gemitibus opem praebens.

64. Quod autem ait: *Quos et vocavit nos non solum ex Iudaeis sed etiam ex gentibus, sicut et in Osee dicit: Vocabo non plebem meam, plebem meam* et cetera, totius huius disputationis propositum ad hoc perducit, ut, quoniam docuit misericordiae dei esse, quod bene operamur, non tamquam ex operibus Iudaei glorientur, qui, cum evangelium percepissent, tamquam meritis suis id tribuendum existimantes nolebant gentibus dari; (2) a qua superbia iam debent desistere intelligentes, quoniam, si non ex operibus sed misericordia dei vocamur, ut credamus, et credentibus praestatur, ut bene operemur, non est gentibus ista invidenda misericordia quasi praelato merito Iudaeorum quod nullum est.

tual men, and is far removed from the wisdom of the flesh. And thus Paul refutes his interlocutor, that he might understand that one should first put away the man of clay in order to deserve to investigate these things by the spirit. (18) And so Paul says, "Who are you, O man, to answer back to God? Does that which is molded say to its molder, 'Why have you made me thus?' Does the potter not have power over the clay, to make out of the same lump a vessel for honor, and another for shame?" (9:20-21). (19) As long as you are a molded thing, says Paul, and you are like this lump of clay, not yet led to spiritual things so that as a spiritual being you might judge all things and be judged by no one, it behooves you to restrain yourself from this sort of inquiry and not to answer back to God. (20) For, appropriately, every one desiring to know God's counsel should first be received into his friendship, a possibility only for spiritual men already bearing the image of the heavenly man. For "then," says the Lord, "I will call you not servants but friends. For everything that I have heard from my father I have made known to you" (Jn 15:15). (21) For as long as you are a potter's vessel, you must first be broken by that iron rod of which it was said: (22) "You will govern them with an iron rod, and you will break them as if they were a potter's vessel" (Ps. 2:9). Then, with the outer man destroyed and the inner man renewed, you might be able, rooted and established in love, to understand the length and breadth and height and depth, to know even the overpowering knowledge of the love of God (Eph. 3:18). (23) So now since from the same lump of clay God has made some vessels for honorable use and some for dishonorable, it is not for you to discuss, whoever you are who still lives according to this lump, that is, who is wise by earthly senses and fleshly wisdom.

63. "God has tolerated with much patience the vessels of wrath made for destruction" (9:22). Here Paul sufficiently indicated that that hardness of heart wrought in Pharaoh had derived deservedly from his preceding hidden impiety. (2) Nonetheless God patiently endured his impiety until at the right time he meted out his punishment. This God did to correct those whom he had decided to free from error, to lead them by calling them back to reverence and piety, offering succour to their prayers and sighs.

64. "We whom he has called not only from the Jews but also from the Gentiles, even as Hosea said: 'I will call those who were not my people my people'" (9:24). This, the theme of the entire argument, here leads to the conclusion, since Paul taught that we do good by the mercy of God, that the Jews should not glory on account of their works, who, when they had received the Gospel, thinking that this should be attributed to their own merit, did not want it to be given to the Gentiles. (2) They ought now to cease from this pridefulness and understand that, if we are called to belief not through our own works but by the mercy of God, so that we who believe do good, then they ought not begrudge the Gentiles this mercy as though it had been given to the Jews on account of their previous merit, which is nothing.

65. Quod autem dicit: *Isaias autem clamat pro Israel: Si fuerit numerus filiorum Israel quasi arena maris, reliquiae salvae fient,* ostendit quemadmodum sit dominus lapis angularis utrumque parietem in se coniungens. (2) Testimonium enim Osee prophetae dictum est pro gentibus: *Vocabo non plebem meam, plebem meam et non dilectam, dilectam;* et Isaiae testimonium dictum pro Israel, quoniam *reliquiae salvae fient,* ut ipsae deputentur in semen Abrahae, quae crediderunt in Christum. (3) Ita concordes ambos populos facit secundum et domini testimonium dicentis in evangelio de gentibus: *Habeo alias oves, quae non sunt de hoc ovili, quas oportet me adducere, et erit unus grex et unus pastor.*

66. Quod autem ait: *Fratres, bona voluntas cordis mei et deprecatio ad deum fit pro illis in salutem,* hinc iam incipit de spe Iudaeorum loqui, ne etiam gentes superbire audeant adversus eos. (2) Sicut enim Iudaeorum superbia refellenda erat tamquam ex operibus gloriantium, sic et gentibus occurrendum est, ne tamquam Iudaeis praelati superbiant.

67. Quod autem dicit: *Prope est verbum in ore tuo et in corde tuo, hoc est verbum fidei, quod praedicamus; quia si confitearis in ore tuo, quia dominus est Iesus, et credideris in corde tuo, quia deus illum suscitavit a mortuis, salvus eris. Corde enim creditur ad iustitiam, ore autem confessio fit in salutem,* (2) totus hic locus ad illud refertur, quod superius dixit: *Verbum enim consummans et brevians faciet dominus super terram.* (3) Remotis enim innumerabilibus et multiplicibus sacramentis, quibus Iudaicus populus premebatur, per misericordiam dei factum est, ut brevitate confessionis fidei ad salutem perveniremus.

68. Quod autem dicit secundum testimonium Moysi: *Ego ad aemulationem vos perducam in non gentem, in gentem insipientem irritabo vos,* dicendo *gentem insipientem* exposuit, quid dixerit: *in non gentem,* quasi quod nec gens dicenda sit, quae insipiens est. (2) De cuius tamen fide irritandum dicit populum Iudaicum, quia illi apprehenderunt, quod isti respuerunt. Vel certe *in non gentem, in gentem insipientem,* quia, cum esset gens insipiens omnis populus idola colens, tamen gentilitatem credendo deposuit. (3) Unde etiam illud est: *Si igitur praeputium iustitiae legis custodiat, nonne praeputium eius in circumcisione deputabitur?* ut sit hic sensus: ego in aemulationem vos adducam in eam, quae non gens facta est, deponendo gentilitatem per fidem Christi, cum fuisset gens insipiens colendo idola.

69. Quod autem ait: *Numquid reppulit deus plebem suam? Absit. Nam et ego Israelita sum ex semine Abraham de tribu Beniamin,* ad hoc refertur, quod superius dixit: (2) *Non potest autem excidere verbum dei. Non enim omnes qui sunt ex Israel, hi sunt Israelitae; neque quia sunt semen*

65. "And Isaiah cries out concerning Israel: 'If the number of the sons of Israel were as the sands of the sea, only a remnant will be saved'" (9:27). This shows how the Lord is the cornerstone, joining both walls in himself. (2) For this is Hosea's testimony on behalf of the Gentiles: "Those who were not my people I will call my people, and those who were not beloved I will call beloved" (Hos. 2:24). And Isaiah says on behalf of Israel, "only a remnant will be saved" (Is. 10:22), that they might be reckoned among those of the seed of Abraham who have believed in Christ. (3) And thus the Lord unites both peoples even as he testified in the Gospel, saying to the Gentiles: "I have other sheep that are not of this fold, whom it is fitting that I lead, and there will be one flock and one shepherd" (Jn 10:16).

66. "Brethren, my heart's desire and my prayer to God for them is that they might be saved" (10:1). Here Paul begins to speak of his hope for the Jews, lest the Gentiles in their turn dare to grow haughty toward them. (2) For just as he had had to refute the pride of the Jews because they gloried in their works, so also with the Gentiles, lest they wax proud as if they had been preferred over the Jews.

67. "The word is near, in your mouth and in your heart, that is, the word of faith which we preach. Because if you confess with your mouth that Jesus is Lord, and if you believe in your heart that God has raised him from the dead, you will be saved. For man believes with his heart and is justified, and confesses with his mouth and is saved" (10:8-10). (2) All this refers to what Paul said above: "For the Lord, with speed and dispatch, will accomplish his Word upon the earth" (9:28). (3) For the innumerable and multitudinous rites which had oppressed the Jewish people have been removed, so that through the mercy of God by the brevity of the confession of faith we might attain salvation.

68. He then says, quoting Moses, "I will make you jealous of those who are not a people, with a foolish people I will make you angry" (10:19). By calling a people "foolish," he explained what he meant by "who are not a people," as though a foolish people ought not be called a people. (2) Yet he says that this people's faith will anger the Jews, because they have accepted what the Jews rejected. Or, surely, Paul says "a non-people," "a foolish people," because even though the people were foolish, given over entirely to idolatry, nonetheless they put away their gentleness by believing. (3) Whence Paul said, "If the uncircumcised keeps the precepts of the Law, will he not be regarded as circumcised?" (2:26). And hence he means, "I will make you jealous of those who once were not a people but who were made a people," for although they had been foolish because of idolatry, they put aside their gentleness through faith in Christ.

69. "Has God rejected his people? By no means! For I myself am an Israelite, a descendant of Abraham, of the tribe of Benjamin" (11:1). This refers to what Paul said above: (2) "The word of God cannot fail. For not all who are from Israel are Israelites, nor because they are descended from

Abraham, omnes filii; sed in Isaac vocabitur tibi semen, (3) ut de ipso scilicet populo Iudaeorum illi deputentur in semen, qui domino crediderunt. De hoc item dicit superius: *Reliquiae salvae fient.*

70. Quod autem dicit: *Dico ergo, numquid sic deliquerunt, ut caderent? Absit. Sed illorum delicto salus gentibus,* non ideo dicit, quia non ceciderunt, sed quia casus ipsorum non fuit inanis, quoniam ad salutem gentium profecit. (2) Non ergo ita deliquerunt, ut caderent, id est, tantummodo ut caderent, quasi ad poenam suam solum, sed ut hoc ipsum, quod ceciderunt, prodesset gentibus ad salutem. (3) Deinde incipit ex hoc loco Iudaeorum populum commendare etiam de ipso casu infidelitatis, ut non superbiant gentes, quia etiam casus Iudaeorum tam pretiosus extitit pro salute gentium, sed magis debent cavere gentes, ne dum superbiunt, similiter cadant.

71. Quod autem ait: *Si esurierit inimicus tuus, ciba illum, si sitit, potum da illi. Hoc enim faciens carbones ignis congeres super caput eius,* multis videri potest repugnare illi sententiae, qua dominus praecepit, ut diligamus inimicos nostros et oremus pro his, qui nos persequuntur, vel huic etiam, quam idem apostolus superius dixit: (2) *Benedicite persequentes vos, benedicite et nolite maledicere,* et iterum: *Nulli malum pro malo reddentes.* Quomodo enim quisque diligit eum cui propterea cibum et potum dat, ut carbones ignis congerat super caput eius, si carbones ignis hoc loco aliquam gravem poenam significant? (3) Quapropter intelligendum est ad hoc dictum esse, ut eum, qui nos laeserit, provocemus ad poenitentiam facti sui, cum ei nos benefacimus. (4) Isti enim carbones ignis ad exustionem id est contribulationem spiritus valent, qui est quasi caput animae, in qua exuritur omnis malitia, cum homo in melius per poenitentiam commutatur, ut sunt illi carbones ignis, de quibus dicitur in psalmis: *Quid detur tibi aut quid apponatur tibi ad linguam subdolam? Sagittae potentis acutae cum carbonibus vastatoribus.*

72. Quod autem ait: *Omnis anima potestatibus sublimioribus subdita sit: non est enim potestas nisi a deo,* rectissime admonet, ne quis ex eo, quod a domino suo in libertatem vocatus est factus christianus, extollatur in superbiam et non arbitretur in huius vitae itinere servandum esse ordinem suum et potestatibus sublimioribus, quibus pro tempore rerum temporalium gubernatio tradita est, putet non se esse subdendum. (2) Cum enim constemus ex anima et corpore et, quamdiu in hac vita temporali sumus, etiam rebus temporalibus ad subsidium degendae huius vitae utamur, oportet nos ex ea parte, quae ad hanc vitam pertinet, subditos esse potestatibus, id est, hominibus res humanas cum aliquo honore administrantibus. (3) Ex illa vero parte, qua credimus deo et in regnum eius vocamur, non nos oportet esse subditos cuiquam homini idipsum in nobis evertere cupienti, quod deus ad vitam aeternam donare dignatus est. (4) Si quis ergo putat, quoniam christianus est, non sibi esse vectigal reddendum aut tributum aut non esse exhibendum honorem debitum eis, qui haec curant

Abraham are they sons of Abraham, but 'through Isaac will your descendants be named'" (9:6-7), (3) so that indeed they from among the Jews will be reckoned as descendants who have believed in the Lord. This is why he says above, "a remnant will be saved."

70. "So I say, have they sinned so as to fall? By no means! But by their trespass salvation has come to the Gentiles" (11:11). Paul does not say that the Jews have not fallen, but that their fall was not in vain, since it profited the Gentiles by salvation. (2) Thus they did not sin so as to fall, that is, only to fall as a punishment, but so that this fall itself would be profitable to the Gentiles for salvation. (3) Thereafter he even begins to praise the Jewish people for this fall of unfaithfulness, so that the Gentiles might not be proud, since this fall of the Jews was so precious for their salvation. Rather, the Gentiles ought to take heed all the more lest, when they grow proud, they likewise fall.

71. "If your enemy is hungry, feed him; if he thirsts, give him drink; For by doing so you will heap coals of fire upon his head" (12:20). This can seem to many people to contradict the Lord's teaching that we should love our enemies and pray for our persecutors (cf. Mt 5:44), or the Apostle's own earlier statement, (2) "Bless those persecuting you, bless them and do not curse them" (12:14), and again, "Return no one evil for evil" (12:17). For how can anyone love someone he feeds and nourishes in order to heap coals of fire upon his head, if "coals of fire" here means some serious penalty? (3) Wherefore one must understand that this means: so that we might stir our persecutor to repentance when we do him a good turn. (4) For these coals of fire serve to burn, that is, to anguish his spirit, which is as it were the head of the soul, from which a man's repentant improvement burns out all maliciousness. And the Psalms speak of these coals of fire: "What should be given to you or what appointed to you for your deceitful tongue? Sharp arrows of the warrior with devouring burning coals" (Ps. 119:3-4).

72. "Let every soul be subject to the higher authorities, for there is no authority except from God" (13:1). Most rightly Paul warns lest anyone, because his Lord has called him to liberty and made him a Christian, be exalted by pride. And let him not suppose that in this life's journey he should not keep his place, nor let him suppose he ought not be subordinate to those higher authorities who, for the time being, may govern temporal things. (2) For we are both soul and body, and however long we exist in this temporal life, we use temporal things to support it. Thus it behooves us in our temporal, physical aspect to be subject to the authorities, that is, to the men who administer human affairs in some office. (3) But concerning our spiritual selves, by which we believe in God and are called into his kingdom, we should not submit to any man desiring to destroy that very thing in us through which God deigned to give us eternal life. (4) Therefore if anyone thinks that since he is a Christian he should not have to pay taxes or tribute, nor to show the respect due those authorities who look

potestatibus, in magno errore versatur. (5) Item si quis sic se putat esse subdendum, ut etiam in suam fidem habere potestatem arbitretur eum, qui temporalibus administrandis aliqua sublimitate praecellit, in maiorem errorem labitur. Sed modus iste servandus est, quem dominus ipse praescribit, ut reddamus Caesari quae sunt Caesaris, et deo quae dei sunt. (6) Quamquam enim ad illud regnum vocemur, ubi nulla erit potestas huius mundi, in hoc tamen itinere dum agimus, donec perveniamus ad illud saeculum, ubi fit evacuatio omnis principatus et potestatis, conditionem nostram pro ipso rerum humanarum ordine toleremus nihil simulate facientes et in eo ipso non tam hominibus quam deo, qui haec iubet, obtemperantes.

73. Quod autem ait: *Vis autem non timere potestatem? bonum fac et habebis laudem ex illa,* potest movere aliquos, cum cogitaverint ab istis potestatibus persecutionem saepe passos fuisse christianos. (2) Numquid ergo non faciebant bonum, quia non solum non sunt laudati ab istis potestatibus, sed etiam poenis affecti et necati sunt? Consideranda ergo sunt verba appostoli. Non enim ait: bonum fac et laudabit te potestas, sed ait: *bonum fac et habebis laudem ex illa.* (3) Sive enim probet factum tuum bonum sive persequatur: *laudem habebis ex illa,* vel cum eam in obsequium dei lucratus fueris vel cum eius persecutione coronam merueris. (4) Hoc etiam in consequentibus intelligitur cum dicit: *Dei enim minister est tibi in bonum,* etiam si sibi in malum.

74. Quod autem ait: *Ideoque necessitate subditi estote,* ad hoc valet, ut intelligamus, quia necesse est propter hanc vitam subditos nos esse oportere non resistentes, si quid illi auferre voluerint, in quod sibi potestas data est, temporalibus rebus, quae quoniam transeunt ideo et ista subiectio non in bonis quasi permansuris sed in necessariis huic tempori constituenda est. (2) Tamen quoniam dixit: *Necessitate subditi estote,* ne quis non integro animo et pura dilectione subditus fieret huiusmodi potestatibus addidit dicens: *Non solum propter iram sed etiam propter conscientiam,* id est, non solum ad iram evacuandam, quod potest etiam simulate fieri, sed ut in tua conscientia certus sis illius dilectione te facere, cui subditus fueris iussu domini tui, *qui omnes vult salvos fieri et in agnitionem veritatis venire*—(3) et hoc enim cum diceret apostolus, de ipsis potestatibus agebat, hoc est, quod servis alio loco suadet: *Non ad oculum servientes quasi hominibus placentes,* ut id ipsum, quod subduntur dominis suis, non eos oderint aut fallaciis promereri desiderent.

75. Quod autem dicit: *Qui enim diligit alterum, legem implevit,* ostendit consummationem legis in dilectione positam, id est in caritate, (2) unde et dominus in illis duobus

after these things, he errs greatly. (5) And likewise if anyone thinks he ought to be so submissive that he holds some officer superior to him in administering temporal matters as authoritative even over his faith, he lapses into greater error. But one ought to serve as the Lord himself prescribes, by rendering to Caesar what is Caesar's and to God what is God's (Mt 22:21). (6) For even though we are called into that kingdom where there will be no temporal authority, nonetheless, while we are on this journey, until we have reached that world where every principality and power will be voided, let us endure our condition for the sake of everyday social order, doing nothing falsely and rendering obedience not so much to men as to God, who commands these things.

73. "Do you want not to fear authority? Then do what is good and you will have praise of him" (13:3). This can provoke some people, because they know that Christians have often suffered persecution at the hands of these authorities. (2) "Therefore," they say, "were these Christians not doing good? For not only did these authorities not praise them, but they punished them and killed them." One must consider the Apostle's words, for he does not say "Do what is good and the authority will praise you," but: "do what is good and you will have praise of him." (3) Thus whether the authority approves your good deed or persecutes you, "You will have praise of him," either when you win it by your allegiance to God, or when you earn the crown of martyrdom by persecution. (4) The subsequent passage should be understood in the same way, when Paul says, "For he is God's servant for your good" (13:4), though it be for his own evil.

74. "And so you must be subject" (13:5). This helps us understand that it is necessary because of this life that we be subject, and that we should not resist anyone wishing to take away any material thing from us, for he has been given authority over temporal things. For since these things pass away, this subjection must then be established not with regard to goods which, as it were, endure forever, but only with regard to the necessities of this time. (2) But, lest anyone submit to the authorities halfheartedly and not from pure love, because he said "You must be subject," Paul continues, "not only because of anger but also for the sake of conscience." That is, you should not submit simply to evade the authority's anger, which you could do deceitfully; but you should be submissive knowing surely in your conscience that you do this out of love for him. For you submit at the command of your Lord, "who wishes all to be saved and to come into the knowledge of the truth" (1 Tim. 2:4)—(3) for the Apostle had said this with these same authorities in mind, that is, as he in another place urges servants: "not serving only with your eyes in a manner pleasing to men" (Eph. 6:6), so that in thus submitting to their lords, they should neither hate them nor seek their praise through deceit.

75. "He who loves another fulfills the law" (13:8). Paul teaches that fulfillment of the Law lies in love, that is, in charity. (2) Whence also the Lord says that the whole Law and all the prophets depend upon these two

praeceptis totam legem pendere dicit et omnes prophetas, id est in dilectione dei et proximi. (3) Unde et ipse, qui legem venit implere, dilectionem donavit per spiritum sanctum, ut quod antea timor implere non poterat, caritas postmodum impleret. (4) Inde est et illud eiusdem
5 apostoli: *Plenitudo autem legis caritas,* et illud: *Finis autem praecepti est caritas de corde puro et conscientia bona et fide non ficta.*

76. Quod autem ait: *Et hoc scientes tempus, quia hora est iam nos de somno surgere,* illuc spectat, quod dictum est: *Ecce nunc tempus acceptabile, ecce nunc dies salutis.* Tempus enim evangelii significatur et illa
10 opportunitas salvos faciendi credentes in deum.

77. Quod autem ait: *Et carnis providentiam ne perfeceritis in concupiscentiis,* ostendit non esse culpandam carnis providentiam, quando ea providentur quae ad necessitatem salutis corporalis valent. (2) Si autem ad superfluas delectationes atque luxurias, ut quisque in his gau-
15 deat, quae carne cupit, recte reprehenditur, quia providentiam carnis in concupiscentiis facit, *quoniam qui seminat in carne sua, de carne metet corruptionem,* id est, qui delectationibus carnalibus gaudet.

78. Quod autem dicit: *Infirmum autem in fide recipite, non in diiudicationibus cogitationum,* hoc dicit ut eum, qui infirmus in fide est, recipi-
20 amus et nostra firmitate infirmitatem eius sustineamus neque diiudicemus cogitationes eius, id est, quasi ferre audeamus sententiam de alieno corde, quod non videmus. (2) Ideo sequitur et dicit: *Alius quidem credit manducare omnia; qui autem infirmus est, olus manducet,* quia illo iam tempore multi iam firmi in fide et scientes secundum sen-
25 tentiam domini non commaculare ea, quae in os intrant, sed quae exeunt, indifferenter sumebant cibos salva conscientia. Quidam vero infirmiores abstinebant a carnibus et a vino, ne vel nescientes inciderent in ea, quae idolis sacrificabantur. (3) Omnis enim tunc immolaticia caro in macello venumdabatur et de primitiis vini libabant
30 gentes simulacris suis et quaedam in ipsis torcularibus sacrificia faciebant. (4) Iubet ergo apostolus et his, qui salva conscientia talibus alimentis utebantur, non spernere infirmitatem illorum, qui se a talibus cibis et potu abstinebant, et illis infirmis, ne eos, qui carnibus vescebantur et vinum bibebant, tamquam pollui iudicarent. (5) Ad hoc
35 valet, quod consequenter dicit: *Qui manducat, non manducantem non iudicet, hoc est spernat, et qui non manducat, manducantem non iudicet.* Firmi enim infirmiores contumaciter contemnebant et infirmi firmos temere iudicabant.

79. Quod autem dicit: *Tu quis es, qui iudices alienum servum?* ad hoc
40 dicit, ut in his rebus, quae possunt et bono animo fieri et malo, iudicium deo dimittamus nec audeamus de alterius corde, quod non videmus, ferre sententiam. (2) In his vero rebus, quae ita comprehenduntur, ut eas bono et casto animo non posse fieri manifestum sit,

precepts, that is, the love of God and neighbor. (3) And so he who came to fulfill the Law gave love through the Holy Spirit, so that what fear earlier could not fulfill was later fulfilled by love. (4) This is the Apostle's point when he says "the fullness of the Law is love," and, "the end of the Law is the love of a pure heart and good conscience and sound faith" (1 Tim. 1:5).

76. "For you know what time it is, that now is the hour for us to wake from sleep" (13:11). This relates to that other sentence: "Behold, now is the acceptable time, now is the day of salvation" (2 Cor. 6:2). Paul indicates here the time of the Gospel, that occasion for saving those who believe in God.

77. "Make no provision for the flesh in its appetites" (13:14),[4] shows that "provision for the flesh" is not to be condemned when what is provided has to do with the needs of bodily health. (2) But if this concern extends to superfluous delights or luxuries, so that a person enjoys the things the flesh desires, he is rightly chastised. For then he makes provision for the flesh's appetites, and "he who sows in the flesh," that is, who enjoys fleshly pleasures, "will glean corruption in the flesh" (Gal. 6:8).

78. "Receive the man weak in faith not for disputing opinions" (14:1). Paul means that we should receive him to support his weakness by our strength. Nor should we dispute his opinions by, for example, daring to pass judgment on the heart of another, which we do not see. (2) So Paul goes on to say, "One believes he can eat all things, while he who is weak eats only vegetables" (14:2), because at that time many people strong in their faith and knowing the Lord's teaching that what defiles a man is not what enters his mouth but what comes out, were eating all foods indifferently with a clear conscience. But certain weaker ones abstained from flesh and wine, lest they even unknowingly eat foods which had been sacrificed to idols. (3) At that time the Gentiles sold all sacrificed meats in butcher shops and poured the first of the wine as a libation to their idols and made certain offerings in their very wine presses. (4) And so the Apostle ordered those using such foods with a clear conscience not to despise the weakness of those abstaining from such food and drink. And he commanded the weak not to consider those who enjoyed this meat and wine as polluted. (5) Thus he goes on to say: "Let him who eats not spurn him who abstains, and let him who abstains not spurn him who eats" (14:3). For the strong were stubbornly condemning the weaker ones, and the weak were rashly judging the strong.

79. "Who are you to pass judgment on the servant of another?" (14:4). Paul says this so that in those matters which could be done with either good or bad intentions, we leave the judgment to God and do not presume to pass judgment on the heart of another, which we do not see. (2) But in those matters so embraced that obviously they could not have been done

---

4. This is the same verse upon which, in *Conf.* VIII.xii, 29, Augustine has his conversion turn.

non improbatur, si iudicemus. Itaque hoc, quod de cibis dicit, quia ignoratur quo animo fiat, non vult nos esse iudices, sed deum; de illo autem nefario stupro, ubi uxorem patris sui quidam habuerat, praecepit debere iudicari. (3) Non enim poterat ille dicere bono animo se tam immane flagitium commisisse. Ergo quaecumque facta ita manifestantur, ut non possit dici: bono animo feci, iudicanda sunt a nobis; quaecumque autem ita fiunt, ut quo animo fiant, incertum sit, non sunt iudicanda sed reservanda iudicio dei, sicut scriptum est: *Quae occulta sunt, deo; quae autem palam sunt, vobis et filiis vestris.*

80. Quod autem ait: *Alius quidem iudicat alternos dies, alius autem iudicat omnem diem,* sequestrata interim meliore consideratione non de duobus hominibus mihi videtur dictum, sed de homine et deo. (2) Qui enim alternos dies iudicat, homo est. Potest enim hodie aliud, cras aliud iudicare, id est, ut quemcumque hodie malum convictum confessumve damnaverit, cras bonum inveniat, cum se correxerit, vel contra, cum aliquem iustum hodie laudaverit, cras inveniat depravatum. (3) Qui autem iudicat omnem diem, deus est, quia non solum qualis quisque sit sed etiam qualis omni die futurus sit novit. (4) Ergo *unusquisque in suo intellectu abundet,* inquit, id est quantum humano intellectui vel unicuique homini concessum est, tantum audeat iudicare. *Qui sapit,* inquit, *diem, domino sapit,* id est quia hoc ipsum ad praesentem diem bene iudicat, domino sapit. (5) Hoc est autem bene iudicare ad diem, ut noveris de correctione eius non esse desperandum in futurum, de cuius culpa manifesta in praesentia iudicaveris.

81. Quod autem ait: *Beatus qui non iudicat semetipsum in quo probat,* ad id potissimum referendum est, quod superius dixit: *Non ergo blasphemetur bonum nostrum.* (2) Hoc est enim etiam, quod nunc ait ante istam sententiam: *Tu fidem, quam habes penes temetipsum, habe coram deo,* ut quoniam bona est haec fides, qua credimus omnia munda mundis, et in ea fide nos probamus, bene utamur ipso bono nostro, ne forte, cum ad offendiculum infirmorum fratrum eo bono abusi fuerimus, peccemus in fratres et in eo ipso bono nos iudicemus, cum scandalizamus infirmos, in quo bono nos probamus, cum ipsa fides nobis placet.

82. Quod autem ait: *Dico enim Christum ministrum fuisse circumcisionis propter veritatem dei ad confirmandas promissiones patrum, gentes autem super misericordia glorificare deum,* ad hoc dicit, ut intelligant gentes dominum Christum ad Iudaeos esse missum et non superbiant. (2) Iudaeis enim repellentibus, quod ad ipsos missum est, factum est ut et gentibus evangelium praedicaretur, quod et in Actibus apostolorum manifestissime scribitur, cum dicunt apostoli Iudaeis: *Vobis primum oportuit praedicari verbum, sed*

with good and chaste intentions, we are not wrong to pass judgment. So on the one hand, concerning food, since we cannot know the inner attitude of the person eating, Paul would have not us but God be judge. However, concerning that abominable lewdness when a certain man had taken his own father's wife, Paul taught that we ought to judge (1 Cor. 5:1f.). (3) For that man could not possibly say that he had committed such a monstrously disgraceful act with good intentions. And so we must pass judgment on whatever deeds are so obviously perverse that it cannot be said, "I did this with good intentions"; but when intentionality remains ambiguous, we should not judge but rather reserve judgment for God, as it is written: "Those things which are hidden belong to God; and those which are revealed, to you and your sons" (Deut. 29:29).

80. "One judges on every other day, but the other judges every day" (14:5-6). For the time being, barring any better opinion, Paul seems to me to speak here about God and man, not about two men. (2) He who judges on alternate days is man, for he can judge one thing one way today and another tomorrow, and whoever today he will have condemned as bad, tomorrow by proof or confession, having corrected himself, he will find good. And the opposite holds true: although today he has praised one man as just, tomorrow he considers him depraved. (3) But he who judges on all days is the Lord, since he knows the measure of each person not only in the present but also for the future. (4) Therefore Paul says, "Let each one be fully convinced in his own mind" (14:5), that is, let him dare to judge only as much as is conceded to human intelligence, or to his own in particular. "He who minds the day, does so for the Lord" (14:6), that is, when one judges well today he minds the day for the Lord. (5) So if you judge well today, you judge a person for his present manifest faults but do not despair of his future correction.

81. "Blessed is he who does not judge himself for what he approves" (14:22). One should relate this especially to Paul's foregoing statement: "Do not let what is good of ours be blasphemed" (14:16). (2) And just before that sentence he says: "The faith you have within you, keep before God," since this faith is good, and by it we believe that all things are pure to the pure, and we approve ourselves. Let us then use well this good of ours, lest perchance by creating a stumbling block for our weaker brethren we abuse it, and so sin against our brothers. For when we scandalize the weak we condemn ourselves by this very good whereby, when this faith pleases us, we approve ourselves.

82. "For I tell you Christ was a minister of the circumcision, to show God's truth in fulfilling the promises made to the fathers. But the Gentiles glorify God for his mercy" (15:8). Paul says this so that the Gentiles would realize that the Lord Christ had been sent to the Jews, and so would not be proud. (2) Since the Jews rejected his coming, the Gospel was preached to the Gentiles. This stands clearly also in the *Acts of the Apostles*, when the apostles say to the Jews: "It was fitting that the Word be preached first to

quoniam indignos vos iudicastis, ecce convertimus nos ad gentes. (3) Secundum etiam ipsa domini testimonia cum dicit: *Non sum missus nisi ad oves perditas domus Israel,* et iterum: *Non est bonum panem filiorum mittere canibus.* (4) Quod gentes si bene considerent, intelligunt ista sua fide, qua iam credunt omnia munda mundis, non se debere insultare his, si qui forte infirmi ex circumcisione fuerint, qui propter communicationem idolorum nullas omnino carnes attingere audeant.

83. Quod autem dicit: *Ut minister sim Christi Iesu in gentibus consecrans evangelium dei, ut fiat oblatio gentium acceptabilis sanctificata in spiritu sancto,* hoc intelligitur, offerantur gentes deo tamquam acceptabile sacrificium, cum in Christum credentes per evangelium sanctificantur, sicut et superius dicit: (2) *Obsecro itaque vos, fratres per misericordiam dei, ut exhibeatis corpora vestra hostiam vivam, sanctam, deo placentem.*

84. Quod autem ait: *Obsecro vos, fratres, ut intendatis in eos, qui dissensiones et scandala praeter doctrinam, quam vos didicistis, faciunt,* de his intelligitur dicere, de quibus et ad Timotheum scribit dicens: (2) *Sicut rogavi te, ut sustineres Ephesi, cum irem in Macedoniam, ut denuntiares quibusdam ne aliter docerent, neque intenderent fabulis et genealogiis interminatis, quae quaestiones praestant magis quam aedificationem dei quae est in fide,* et ad Titum: (3) *Sunt enim multi non subditi, vaniloqui et mentis seductores, maxime qui ex circumcisione sunt, quos oportet refelli, qui universas domos subvertunt docentes, quae non oportet, turpis lucri gratia; dixit quidam ex ipsis proprius eorum propheta: Cretenses semper mendaces, malae bestiae, ventres pigri.* (4) Ad hoc enim refertur, quod et hic ait: *Hi enim Christo domino non serviunt, sed suo ventri,* de quibus alio loco dicit: *Quorum deus venter est.*

you, but since you have judged yourselves unworthy, behold, we turn to the Gentiles" (Acts 13:46). (3) Moreover, this accords with the Lord's own testimony, when he says, "I was sent only to the lost sheep of the house of Israel" (Mt 15:24), and again, "It is not a good thing for the children's bread to be thrown to the dogs" (Mt 15:26). (4) If the Gentiles consider carefully, they will understand by their very own faith, by which they now believe "all things are pure to the pure," that they ought not insult those converts from Judaism who, perhaps still weak, dare not touch every sort of meat, fearing its contact with idols.

83. "That I may be a minister of Jesus Christ among the Gentiles in priestly service of God's Gospel, so that the offering of the Gentiles might be acceptable, having been sanctified by the Holy Spirit" (15:16). Thus the Gentiles are offered to God as an acceptable sacrifice when, believing in Christ, they are sanctified through the Gospel. As Paul said above: (2) "Thus I appeal to you, brethren, by the mercy of God, to present your bodies as a living sacrifice, holy and pleasing to God" (12:1).

84. "I appeal to you, brethren, that you watch out for those who create dissentions and offenses contrary to the doctrine that you have learned" (16:17). Paul here discusses those people whom he wrote to Timothy about, saying: (2) "As I urged you when I was going to Macedonia, remain at Ephesus, so that you might charge certain people neither to teach a different doctrine nor to engage themselves in thinking about myths and endless genealogies, which promote speculation rather than the edification about God that is in faith" (1 Tim. 1:3,4). And to Titus: (3) "For there are many men who are not submissive; empty talkers, seducers of the mind, Jews for the most part, who ought to be refuted, who upset entire families teaching things they ought not teach for the sake of filthy lucre. A certain one of them, a prophet of their own, has said, 'Cretans are always liars, evil beasts and lazy gluttons'" (Titus 1:10-12). (4) Paul takes up the same point here when he says, "These men do not serve the Lord Christ, but their own belly," and he says of them in another place, "Their belly is their god" (Phil. 3:19).

EPISTOLAE AD ROMANOS
INCHOATA EXPOSITIO

UNFINISHED COMMENTARY ON THE
EPISTLE TO THE ROMANS

EPISTOLAE AD ROMANOS
INCHOATA EXPOSITIO

1. In epistola quam Paulus apostolus scripsit ad Romanos, quantum ex eius textu intelligi potest, quaestionem habet talem, utrum Iudaeis solis evangelium domini nostri Iesu Christi venerit propter merita operum legis, an vero nullis operum meritis praecedentibus omnibus gentibus venerit iustificatio fidei, quae est in Christo Iesu, ut non, quia iusti erant homines, crederent, sed credendo iustificati deinceps iuste vivere inciperent. (2) Hoc ergo docere intendit apostolus omnibus venisse gratiam evangelii domini nostri Iesu Christi. Quam propterea etiam gratiam vocari ostendit, quia non quasi debitum iustitiae redditum est, sed gratuito datum. (3) Coeperant enim nonnulli, qui ex Iudaeis crediderant, tumultuari adversus gentes et maxime adversus apostolum Paulum, quod incircumcisos et a legis veteris vinculis liberos admittebat ad evangelii gratiam praedicans eis, ut in Christum crederent nullo imposito carnalis circumcisionis iugo. (4) Sed plane tanta moderatione, uti nec Iudaeos superbire permittat tamquam de meritis operum legis nec gentes merito fidei adversus Iudaeos inflari, quod ipsi receperint Christum, quem illi crucifixerunt. Tamquam enim sicut alio loco dicit pro ipso domino legatione fungens, hoc est pro lapide angulari, utrumque populum tam ex Iudaeis quam ex gentibus connectit in Christo per vinculum gratiae utrisque auferens omnem superbiam meritorum et iustificandos utrosque per disciplinam humilitatis associans.

2. Itaque epistolam sic exorsus est: *Paulus servus Iesu Christi vocatus apostolus, segregatus in evangelium dei.* Breviter in duobus verbis ecclesiae dignitatem a synagogae vetustate discernit. (2) Ecclesia quippe ex vocatione appellata est, synagoga vero ex congregatione. Convocari enim magis hominibus congruit, congregari autem magis pecoribus, unde etiam greges proprie pecorum dici solent. (3) Quamquam ergo plerisque scripturarum locis ipsa ecclesia grex dei et pecus dei et ovile dei vocetur, tamen cum in comparatione homines pecora dicuntur ad vitam veterem pertinent. (4) Et apparet huiusmodi homines non cibo sempiternae veritatis, sed temporalium promissionum tamquam terreno pabulo esse contentos. *Paulus* ergo *servus Christi Iesu vocatus* est *apostolus*, quae vocatio illum coaptavit ecclesiae. (5) *In evangelium* autem *dei segregatus est*, unde nisi a grege synagogae, si verborum Latinorum significatio omni modo cum Graeca interpretatione concordet.

UNFINISHED COMMENTARY ON THE EPISTLE TO THE ROMANS

1. The letter of Paul the Apostle to the Romans, insofar as one can understand its literal content, poses a question like this: whether the Gospel of our Lord Jesus Christ came to the Jews alone because of their merits through the works of the Law, or whether the justification of faith which is in Christ Jesus came to all nations, without any preceding merits for works. In this last instance, people would believe not because they were just but, justified through belief, they would then begin to live justly. (2) This, then, is what the Apostle intends to teach: that the grace of the Gospel of our Lord Jesus Christ came to all men. He thereby shows why one calls this "grace," for it was given freely, and not as the repayment of a debt of righteousness. (3) For some of the Jewish believers had begun to agitate against the Gentiles and particularly against the apostle Paul, because he admitted the uncircumcised, who were free of the chains of the Old Law, to the grace of the Gospel, and he preached Christ to them without any imposition of the yoke of fleshly circumcision. (4) But clearly Paul teaches this with such moderation that he permits neither the Jews to be proud because of the merits of the Law, nor the Gentiles to be haughty towards the Jews because of the merit of their faith in accepting Christ, whom the Jews crucified. For just as he says elsewhere, discharging the mission of the Lord, the Cornerstone, Paul unites in Christ through the bond of grace peoples from among the Jews and Gentiles both, taking away from both all pride because of merit, and bringing both together to be justified by the discipline of humility (cf. Eph. 2:20).

2. And so he begins his epistle: "Paul the slave of Jesus Christ, called to be an apostle, set apart for the Gospel of God" (1:1). Briefly by these two words, "called" and "set apart," Paul distinguishes the Church's dignity from the desuetude of the synagogue. (2) For indeed the Church is so named because it "calls forth"; the synagogue, because it "gathers together."[1] For "to be called together" is more appropriately said of men, whereas "to be gathered together" is more appropriately said of animals (which is why the word "herds"—that is, "gatherings"—is normally used with particular reference to animals). (3) Therefore, although Scripture in many places calls the Church herself God's flock or herd or sheepfold, nevertheless, when men are compared to cattle, it pertains to the old life. (4) And clearly men of this sort content themselves not with the food of eternal truth but, so to speak, with the earthly fodder of temporal promises. "Paul," then, is "slave of Jesus Christ, called to be an apostle," and thereby joined to the Church. (5) And moreover, he was "set apart for the Gospel of God"—set apart from what, if not the flock of the synagogue?—if the sense of the Latin words accords completely with the meaning of the Greek.

---

1. Two commonplace ecclesiastical Hellenisms. *Ecclesia* (ἐκκλησία) derives from καλέω ("to call"), stem—κλη; synagogue from συνάγω ("to bring together").

3. Sane evangelium dei, in quod segregatum se esse commemorat, commendat auctoritate prophetarum, ut, quoniam credentes in Christum, in quorum numerum vocatus est, Iudaeis praeposuerat, a quibus se dixerat segregatum, gentes rursus iam non superbire admoneat, (2) siquidem de populo Iudaeorum fuerunt prophetae, per quos evangelium, cuius fide credentes iustificantur, ante promissum esse testatur. *Segregatus* enim inquit, *in evangelium dei, quod ante promiserat per prophetas suos.* (3) Fuerunt enim et prophetae non ipsius, in quibus etiam aliqua inveniuntur, quae de Christo audita cecinerunt, sicut etiam de Sibylla dicitur; quod non facile crederem, nisi quod poetarum quidam in Romana lingua nobilissimus, antequam diceret ea de innovatione saeculi, quae in domini nostri Iesu Christi regnum satis concinere et convenire videantur, praeposuit versum dicens:

Ultima Cumaei iam venit carminis aetas.

(4) Cumaeum autem carmen sibyllinum esse nemo dubitaverit. Sciens ergo apostolus ea in libris gentium inveniri testimonia veritatis, quod etiam in Actibus Apostolorum loquens Atheniensibus manifestissime ostendit, non solum ait: *per prophetas suos,* (5) ne quis a pseudoprophetis per quasdam veritatis confessiones in aliquam impietatem seduceretur, sed addidit etiam: *in scripturis sanctis,* volens utique ostendere litteras gentium superstitiosae idolatriae plenissimas non ideo sanctas haberi oportere, quia in eis aliquid, quod ad Christum pertinet, invenitur.

4. Et ne quisquam etiam prophetas aliquos remotos atque alienos a gente Iudaeorum forte praeferret, in quibus nullus simulacrorum cultus esset, quantum attinet ad simulacra, quae humana operatur manus—nam simulacris phantasmatum suorum sectatores suos omnis error illudit—(2) ne quis tamen aliqua huiusmodi praeferens, quia ibi Christi nomen ostentat, eas potius sanctas scripturas esse asserat, non eas, quae populo Hebraeorum sunt divinitus creditae, satis opportune mihi videtur adiungere, cum dixisset: *in scripturis sanctis,* quod adiecit: *de filio suo, qui factus est ei ex semine David secundum carnem.* (3) David enim certe rex Iudaeorum fuit. Oportebat autem, ut ex illa gente orirentur Christi praenuntiatores prophetae, ex qua gente carnem assumpturus erat, quem praenuntiabant. (4) Occurrendum autem erat etiam illorum impietati, qui dominum nostrum Iesum Christum secundum hominem tantummodo, quem suscepit, accipiunt, divinitatem autem in eo non intelligunt ab universae creaturae communione discretam, velut ipsi Iudaei, qui Christum filium tantummodo David esse opinabantur ignorantes excellentiam, qua dominus est ipsius David secundum id, quod est filius dei. (5) Unde illos in evangelio redarguit per prophetiam, quae ipsius David ore prolata est. (6) Quaerit enim ab eis, quem ipse David dominum appellat, quomodo filius eius sit, cui

3. Quite rightly he commends the Gospel of God, for which he says he had been set apart, by the authority of the prophets. He does this to caution the Gentiles, into whose ranks as believers in Christ he had been called and whom he had placed before the Jews from whom he had been set apart, not to be proud in their turn, (2) inasmuch as the prophets had arisen from the Jewish people, and Paul testifies that the Gospel, in which believers are justified by faith, had been promised earlier through them. For he says, "I have been set apart for the Gospel of God, which he had promised beforehand through his prophets" (1:2). (3) For there are alien prophets as well, in whom also are found some things which they heard of Christ and prophesied. This sort of thing is said even about the Sibyl, which I would not readily credit were it not for one of the poets, the greatest in the Roman language. This poet, before describing the renewal of the world in a way which seems to harmonize and accord well with the kingdom of our lord Jesus Christ, prefaced a verse by saying:

The last age prophesied by the Cumaean song has now come.
(Vergil, Eclogues 4,4)

(4) And everyone knows that the "Cumaean song" is the Sybil's. Therefore the Apostle, knowing that the books of the Gentiles contain these witnesses to the truth (as he also most clearly showed in the *Acts of the Apostles* when speaking to the Athenians [Acts 17:28]), not only said "through God's own prophets," (5) (lest anyone be seduced into some impiety by the witness to the truth found in false prophets), but he also added "in the Holy Scriptures," wishing undoubtedly to show that the writings of the Gentiles, so very full of superstitious idolatry, ought not be considered holy just because they say something about Christ.

4. Furthermore, lest anyone put forward any prophets foreign to the Jews, who worshipped no idols—at least, no idols made by human hands: for every error deceives its followers by the images of its own imaginings—(2) lest anyone, notwithstanding, put forth this sort of argument, because these other prophets declare the name of Christ, that they rather are the sacred scriptures, and not those which were divinely entrusted to the Hebrew people, quite appropriately, it seems to me, Paul, after saying "in the Holy Scriptures," adds: "concerning his son, who was made from the seed of David according to the flesh" (1:3). (3) For David was certainly the king of the Jews. Moreover, it was fitting that the prophets, who foretold the coming of Christ, arise among that people from whom he himself assumed flesh, as they had predicted. (4) Paul also had to oppose the impiety of those who accept our Lord Jesus Christ only according to the man whom he put on, but do not comprehend his divinity, which sets him apart from every other creature. They are like the Jews themselves who thought that Christ was the son of David only, ignorant of that preeminence by which he is the Lord of David himself, because he is the Son of God. (5) Thus Christ in the Gospel refutes them by this same David's prophecy. (6) For he asks them how the person David calls "Lord" could be David's

deberent utique respondere, quod secundum carnem filius esset David, secundum divinitatem autem filius dei et dominus ipsius David. (7) Quod Paulus apostolus quia iam didicerat, posteaquam dixit: *in evangelium dei, quod ante promiserat per prophetas suos in scripturis sanctis de filio suo, qui factus est ei ex semine David,* addidit: *secundum carnem,* ne hoc solum et totum in Christo esse arbitrarentur, quod factum erat secundum carnem. (8) Addendo ergo: *secundum carnem* servavit divinitati dignitatem suam. Quae non solum semini David, sed nec alicui angelicae aut cuiusvis excellentissimae creaturae generationi tribui potest, quandoquidem ipsum est verbum dei, per quod facta sunt omnia. (9) Quod verbum ex semine David secundum carnem factum est et habitavit in nobis non mutatum et conversum in carnem, sed carne, ut carnalibus congruenter appareret, indutum. (10) Quapropter apostolus non solum eo verbo, quod ait: *secundum carnem,* humanitatem a divinitate distinxit, sed etiam illo, quod ait: *factus est.* Non est enim factus secundum id, quod verbum dei est. (11) Omnia enim per ipsum facta sunt, nec fieri cum omnibus posset, per quem facta sunt omnia. Neque ante omnia factus est, ut per ipsum fierent omnia. Ipso enim excepto, si ante illa iam factus esset, non essent illa omnia, quae per illum fierent, nec possent vere dici facta omnia per ipsum, in quibus ipse non esset, si ipse etiam factus esset. (12) Et ideo apostolus, cum factum diceret Christum, addidit: *secundum carnem,* ut secundum verbum, quod est filius dei, non factum a deo, sed natum esse monstraret.

5. Eundem sane ipsum, *qui secundum carnem factus est ex semine David, praedestinatum* dicit *filium dei in virtute,* non secundum carnem, sed *secundum spiritum,* nec quemlibet spiritum, sed *spiritum sanctificationis ex resurrectione mortuorum.* (2) In resurrectione enim virtus morientis apparet, ut diceretur: *praedestinatus in virtute secundum spiritum sanctificationis ex resurrectione mortuorum.* Deinde sanctificatio vitam novam fecit, quae domini nostri resurrectione signata est. (3) Unde idem apostolus alio loco dicit: *Si consurrexistis cum Christo, quae sursum sunt quaerite, ubi Christus est in dextera dei sedens.* (4) Potest quidem etiam sic esse ordo verborum, ut non ad *spiritum sanctificationis* adiungamus quod ait: *ex resurrectione mortuorum,* sed ad id quod ait: *praedestinatus est,* ut ordo sit: *qui praedestinatus est ex resurrectione mortuorum,* cui ordini interposita sunt haec: *filius dei in virtute secundum spiritum sanctificationis.* (5) Et nimirum iste ordo certior et melior videtur, ut sit filius David in infirmitate secundum carnem, filius autem dei in virtute secundum spiritum sanctificationis. (6) *Factus est* ergo *ex semine David,* id est

son, and to this they certainly should have responded that he was the son of David according to the flesh, but according to his divinity, the Son of God and Lord of this same David. (7) Hence Paul the Apostle, because he already knew this, said, "for the Gospel of God, which he promised beforehand through his own prophets in the Holy Scriptures concerning his Son, who was descended from the seed of David," and then added, "according to the flesh," lest they think that this fleshly descent exhausted Christ's significance. (8) By thus adding "according to the flesh," Paul preserved the honor of Christ's divinity, which can be attributed neither to the seed of David nor to any angel nor to the generation of whatever most excellent creature you please, for this divinity is the Word of God through whom all things were made. (9) This Word according to the flesh was made from the seed of David and dwelt among us, not changed and turned into flesh, but clothed with flesh in order fittingly to be visible to the fleshly. (10) And so the Apostle distinguished Christ's humanity from his divinity by saying, "according to the flesh," and also by saying "was made." For Christ was not created or made insofar as he is the Word of God. (11) For all things, rather, were made through him (Jn 1:3), nor could he through whom all things were made have been made along with all things. Nor was he made before all things, so that through him all things except himself were made. If he had been made before them, then those things which were made by him would not be "all things," nor could "all things" rightly be said to have been made by him since he himself would not be included if he had himself indeed been made. (12) And thus the Apostle, when he said Christ was "made" or "born," added, "according to the flesh": for insofar as he is the Word, the Son of God, he was not made by God, as Paul makes clear, but begotten by him.

5. And this same one who "according to the flesh was born of the seed of David" Paul calls "predestined Son of God in power," not according to the flesh, but "according to the Spirit," and not just any spirit, but the "Spirit of sanctification by the resurrection of the dead" (1:3-4). (2) For in the resurrection appears the power of Christ who died, so that it might be said: "predestined in power according to the Spirit of sanctification by the resurrection of the dead" (1:4). Thereafter sanctification achieved new life, which is signified in our Lord's resurrection. (3) And so this same Apostle says elsewhere: "If you have arisen with Christ, seek the things that are above where Christ is, sitting at the right hand of God" (Col. 3:1). (4) The word order here could be such that we might connect "by the resurrection of the dead" not to "the Spirit of sanctification" but to "he was predestined." The order then would be: "who was predestined by the resurrection of the dead"; and interpolated into this order were the following words: "Son of God in power according to the Spirit of sanctification." (5) This word order seems surer and better, so that Christ is the son of David in weakness according to the flesh, but Son of God in power according to the Spirit of sanctification. (6) "For he was born of the seed of David" (1:3), that is, the

filius David ex mortali corpore, propter quod et mortuus est. *Praedestinatus est* autem *filius dei* et dominus ipsius David *ex resurrectione mortuorum*. (7) In quantum enim mortuus est, ad id pertinet, quod est filius David, in quantum autem resurrexit a mortuis, ad id, quod est
5 filius dei et dominus ipsius David, sicut alibi idem apostolus dicit: *Nam etsi mortuus est ex infirmitate, sed vivit in virtute dei,* ut infirmitas pertineat ad David, vita vero aeterna ad virtutem dei. (8) Ideoque in his ipsis verbis dominum suum designat eum David dicens: *Dixit dominus domino meo: Sede ad dexteram meam, donec ponam inimicos tuos sub*
10 *pedibus tuis.* (9) Ex eo enim, quod resurrexit a mortuis, sedet ad dexteram patris. Praedestinatum ergo ex resurrectione mortuorum, ut sederet ad dexteram patris, videns in spiritu David non auderet dicere filium suum sed dominum suum. (10) Unde et consequenter apostolus hic adiungit: *Iesu Christi domini nostri,* posteaquam dixit: *ex resurrectione*
15 *mortuorum* et tamquam admonens, unde illum David dominum suum potius quam filium esse testatus sit. (11) Non autem ait eum praedestinatum ex resurrectione a mortuis, sed *ex resurrectione mortuorum.* Non enim resurrectione ipsa sua filius apparet dei propria illa et eminentissima dignitate, qua iam caput est ecclesiae, cum et ceteri mor-
20 tui resurrecturi sint, sed filius dei praedestinatus est quodam principatu resurrectionis, quia ex resurrectione omnium mortuorum ipse praedestinatus est, id est ut prae ceteris et ante ceteros resurgeret designatus, ut, quod hic positum est: *Filius dei,* cum dixisset: *praedestinatus est,* ad documentum valeat tantae sublimitatis. (12) Non enim sic praede-
25 stinari oportuit nisi filium dei, secundum quod est etiam caput ecclesiae, unde illum alio loco primogenitum ex mortuis appellat. (13) Eum enim decebat venire ad iudicium resurgentium, qui praecesserat ad exemplum, neque ad exemplum omnium resurgentium sed ad exemplum eorum, qui sic resurrecturi sunt, ut cum illo vivant et reg-
30 nent in sempiternum, quorum etiam caput est tamquam corporis sui. Ex ipsorum enim resurrectione etiam praedestinatus est, ut ipsis princeps fieret, ceterorum autem in sua conditione resurgentium non princeps, sed iudex est. (14) Non itaque ex illorum mortuorum resurrectione praedestinatus est, quos est damnaturus. Praedestinatum enim
35 esse ex resurrectione mortuorum, ut praecederet resurrectionem mortuorum, vult intelligi apostolus; hos autem praecessit, qui ad ipsum caeleste regnum, quo eos praecessit, secuturi sunt. (15) Propter quod non ait: qui praedestinatus est filius dei ex resurrectione mortuorum Iesus Christus dominus noster, sed: *ex resurrectione mortuorum Iesu*
40 *Christi domini nostri,* tamquam si diceret: qui praedestinatus est filius dei ex resurrectione mortuorum suorum, hoc est, ad se pertinentium in vitam aeternam, velut si interrogaretur: quorum mortuorum? et responderet: ipsius Iesu Christi domini nostri. (16) Ex resurrectione enim ceterorum mortuorum non est praedestinatus, quos non praeces-
45 sit ad gloriam vitae aeternae, non utique secuturos, quoniam ad poenas suas impii resurrecturi sunt. (17) Ergo ille tamquam filius dei unigenitus

son of David by his mortal body, because of which he also died. But he was "predestined Son of God" and Lord of this same David "by the resurrection of the dead." (7) His death pertains to his status as son of David; his resurrection from the dead, to his status as the Son of God and Lord of that same David, as elsewhere the same Apostle says: "For he died in weakness, yet he lives by the power of God" (2 Cor. 13:4). Thus weakness relates to David, but life eternal to the power of God. (8) And by these very words David designates him his own Lord, saying: "The Lord said to my Lord, 'sit at my right hand, until I put your enemies beneath your feet'" (Ps. 109:1). (9) In rising from the dead, he sits at the right hand of the Father. Therefore David, inspired, seeing that Christ was predestined by the resurrection of the dead to sit at the right hand of the Father, did not dare to call him his own son, but said instead, "My Lord." (10) Consequently the Apostle, after saying "by the resurrection of the dead," adds, "of Jesus Christ our Lord," as though indicating why David had declared that Christ was his Lord rather than his son. (11) Moreover, Paul does not say that Christ was predestined by *his* resurrection *from* the dead, but "by *the* resurrection *of* the dead." For his own resurrection does not show how he is the Son of God, and by this special and most outstanding worthiness the head of the Church, since others also will be raised from the dead. But he was predestined Son of God by a certain primacy of resurrection, since he himself was predestined by the resurrection of all the dead; that is, he was appointed to rise above and before the others, so that when Paul adds "the Son of God" to "predestined," this serves as proof of such great sublimity. (12) For the Son of God alone was appropriately so predestined, according to which he is also the head of the Church, and for this reason Paul elsewhere calls him the first-born from the dead (Col. 1:18). (13) For Christ properly comes to judge others rising from the dead, as he had preceded them as an exemplar. An exemplar, furthermore, not of all who rise but of those who will be resurrected so that they live and reign with him for eternity, for he is the head and they are like his body. By their resurrection was he predestined, to become their leader; but in his resurrected state he does not lead the others, but judges them. (14) For he was not predestined by the resurrection of those dead whom he will condemn: by "predestined by the resurrection of the dead," the Apostle wants "preceded the resurrection of the dead" to be understood, for Christ goes before those who will follow him into the heavenly kingdom. (15) And so in light of this Paul does not say "who was predestined Son of God by the resurrection of the dead, Jesus Christ our Lord." Rather, he says, "who was predestined Son of God by the resurrection of the dead *of* Jesus Christ our Lord," as though he had said, "by the resurrection of his own dead," that is, of those who belong to him in life eternal. It is as if he had been asked "Which dead?" and answered, "of Jesus Christ our Lord himself." (16) For he was not predestined by the resurrection of those other dead whom he did not precede into the glory of eternal life and who certainly will not follow him, since the impious will be resurrected for their own punishment. (17) Therefore he, as only-begotten

etiam primogenitus ex mortuis *praedestinatus est ex resurrectione mortuorum.* Quorum mortuorum, nisi *Iesu Christi domini nostri?*

6. *Per quem accepimus,* inquit, *gratiam et apostolatum,* gratiam cum omnibus fidelibus, apostolatum autem non cum omnibus. Et ideo si tantummodo apostolatum se diceret accepisse, ingratus extitisset gratiae qua illi peccata dimissa sunt. Tamquam enim meritis priorum operum accepisse apostolatum videretur. (2) Optime itaque tenet cardinem causae, ut nemo audeat dicere vitae prioris meritis se ad evangelium esse perductum, quando nec ipsi apostoli, qui ceteris membris post caput corporis supereminent, accipere apostolatum proprie potuissent, nisi prius communiter cum ceteris gratiam, quae peccatores sanat et iustificat, accepissent. (3) Quod autem subiungit: *Ad oboediendum fidei in omnibus gentibus pro nomine eius,* ad hoc dicit apostolatum se accepisse, ut oboediatur fidei pro nomine domini nostri Iesu Christi, hoc est ut credant omnes Christo et signentur in eius nomine qui salvi esse cupiunt. (4) Quam salutem non solis Iudaeis, sicut nonnulli, qui ex ipsis crediderant, arbitrabantur, venisse iam ostendit cum ait: *in omnibus gentibus, in quibus estis,* inquit, *et vos vocati Iesu Christi,* id est ut et vos sitis eius Iesu Christi, qui omnium gentium salus est, quamquam non in numero Iudaeorum, sed in numero ceterarum gentium sitis inventi.

7. Huc usque dixit ipse, quis esset qui scribit epistolam. Est enim qui scribit epistolam *Paulus servus Iesu Christi, vocatus apostolus, segregatus in evangelium dei.* (2) Sed quia occurrebat: Quod evangelium? respondit: *quod ante promiserat per prophetas suos in scripturis sanctis de filio suo.* Item quia occurrebat: De quo filio suo? respondit: *qui factus est ei ex semine David secundum carnem, qui praedestinatus est filius dei in virtute secundum spiritum sanctificationis ex resurrectione mortuorum Iesu Christi domini nostri.* (3) Et quasi diceretur: Quomodo tu ad eum pertines? respondit: *per quem accepimus gratiam et apostolatum ad oboediendum fidei in omnibus gentibus pro nomine eius.* (4) Item quasi diceretur: Quae igitur causa est, ut scribas ad nos? respondit: *in quibus estis et vos vocati Iesu Christi.* (5) Nunc deinde adiungit ex more epistolae quibus scribat: *Omnibus,* inquit, *qui sunt Romae, dilectis dei, vocatis sanctis.* Etiam hic significavit benignitatem dei potius quam meritum illorum. Non enim ait: diligentibus deum, sed: *dilectis dei.* (6) Prior enim dilexit nos ante omnia merita, ut et nos eum dilecti diligeremus. (7) Unde etiam addidit: *vocatis sanctis.* Quamquam enim sibi quis tribuat quod vocanti obtemperat, nemo potest sibi tribuere quod vocatus est. *Vocatis* autem *sanctis* non ita intelligendum est, tamquam ideo vocati sint, quia

Son of God and first-born from the dead, was "predestined by the resurrection of the dead"—of which dead, if not those "of Jesus Christ our Lord"?

6. "Through whom we have received grace and apostleship" (1:5), grace together with all the faithful, but not so apostleship. If Paul were saying that he had received only apostleship, he would have appeared ungrateful for that grace by which his sins had been remitted, and might then seem to have received his apostleship because of the merits of his prior works. (2) Thus very well does Paul preserve the main point of his case so that no one dare say that he has been led to the Gospel because of the merits of his prior life. How could one claim this, when even the apostles themselves, who tower above the other members of the body of the Church after Christ the Head, could not have received their own apostleship unless first together with these other members of the Church they had received grace, which cleanses and justifies sinners? (3) And so he adds: "to bring about the obedience of faith in all nations for his name." That is, Paul says that he had received apostleship so that he might submit to the faith in the name of our Lord Jesus Christ, so that everyone desiring to be saved might believe in Christ and be sealed in his name. (4) Paul teaches here that this salvation had come not only to the Jews, as some Jewish Christians thought, when he says: "in all the nations, among whom are you also who are called to belong to Jesus Christ" (1:6). That is, so that you also are Jesus Christ's, the Salvation of all the nations, even though you have been found not among the Jews, but among other peoples.

7. So far he has simply introduced himself as the author of this letter: "Paul, a slave of Jesus Christ, called to be an apostle, set apart for the Gospel of God." (2) But because the question occurred: What gospel? he answered, "which he had promised beforehand through his prophets in the Holy Scriptures concerning his son." And since again the question occurred: What son? he answered, "who was born to him of the seed of David according to the flesh, who was predestined Son of God in power according to the Spirit of sanctification by the resurrection of the dead of Jesus Christ our Lord" (1:4). (3) And as though someone had asked: How do you relate to him? Paul answered, "through whom we have received grace and apostleship to bring about the obedience of faith in all nations, for the sake of his name" (1:5). (4) And again, as if someone had asked: Why then do you write to us? he answered, "among whom are you also who are called to belong to Jesus Christ" (1:6). (5) Paul adds next, as one will in a letter, an address: "To all those at Rome, beloved of God, called to be saints." And here again he has emphasized God's benignity rather than their merit. For he did not say, "to those loving God," but "to those beloved of God." (6) For he has loved us first before all merit, so that we, having been loved, would love him. (7) Whereupon Paul adds "to those called to be saints." For although someone might credit himself for submitting to the call, no one can credit himself for having been called. Furthermore, one should not think that "called to be saints" indicates that they were called because they

sancti erant, sed ideo sancti effecti, quia vocati sunt.

8. Restat ergo ut salutem dicat, ut compleatur usitatum epistolae principium, tamquam ille illis salutem. Pro eo autem ac si diceret salutem: *gratia vobis,* inquit, *et pax a deo patre nostro et domino Iesu Christo.* Non enim omnis gratia est a deo. (2) Nam et iudices mali praebent gratiam in accipiendis personis aliqua cupiditate illecti aut timore perterriti. (3) Neque omnis pax dei est vel ab illo, unde ipse dominus discernens ait: *Pacem meam do vobis,* adiungens etiam et dicens non se talem pacem dare qualem dat hic mundus. (4) Gratia est ergo a deo patre et domino Iesu Christo, qua nobis peccata remittuntur, quibus adversabamur deo, pax vero ipsa, qua reconciliamur deo. (5) Cum enim per gratiam remissis peccatis absumptae fuerint inimicitiae, restat ut pace adhaereamus illi, a quo nos sola peccata dirimebant, sicut propheta dicit: (6) *Non gravabit aurem, ut non audiat, sed peccata vestra inter vos et deum separant.* Quibus remissis per fidem domini nostri Iesu Christi nulla separatione interveniente pax erit.

9. Fortasse autem quisque miretur, quomodo intelligenda sit iustitia iudicis dei, cum gratiam praebet ignoscendo peccantibus. (2) Sed hoc plane iustum est apud deum, quia vere iustum est, ut hi, quos peccatorum suorum poenitet, eo tempore, quo nondum poenarum manifestus terror apparet, misericorditer separentur ab eis, qui defensiones peccatorum suorum pertinaciter exquirentes nulla poenitentia corrigi volunt. (3) Iniustum est enim, ut cum his illi ad consortium poenale copulentur, qui vocantem deum non spreverunt et peccantes displicuerunt sibi, ut, quemadmodum ille peccata eorum, sic etiam ipsi odissent sua. (4) Ea enim demum est humanae iustitiae disciplina non in se amare nisi quod dei est, et odisse quod proprium est; nec approbare peccata sua nec in eis alium improbare sed seipsum; nec putare satis sibi esse ut sua peccata displiceant, nisi etiam vigilantissima deinceps intentione vitentur; nec in eis vitandis vires suas existimare sufficere, nisi divinitus adiuvetur. (5) Iustum est ergo apud deum, ut ignoscatur talibus quaecumque antea commiserunt, ne, quod iniustissimum est, cum eis qui tales non sunt, confundantur atque misceantur. (6) Quapropter et quia talibus ignoscitur, iustitia dei est, et quia ignoscitur, gratia est. Iusta est ergo gratia dei et grata iustitia, cum in eo quoque etiam poenitentiae meritum gratia praecedat, quod neminem peccati sui poeniteret nisi admonitione aliqua vocationis dei.

10. Porro iustitiae divinae tanta constantia est, ut cum poena spiritualis et sempiterna poenitenti fuerit relaxata, pressurae tamen cruciatusque corporales, quibus etiam

were holy. Rather, they were made holy because they were called.

8. Only the salutation remains to complete the customary opening of a letter, like "X to Y, greetings."[2] Instead of saying "greetings," Paul says, "Grace to you and peace from God our Father and the Lord Jesus Christ." For not all grace is from God. (2) Even evil judges grant grace when considering a person, having been seduced by some greed or terrified by fear. (3) Nor is all peace God's, or from God, which is why the the Lord himself made the distinction when he said, "My peace I give to you," adding as well that his peace is not the sort that this world gives. (4) Grace then is from God the Father and the Lord Jesus Christ, by which our sins, which had turned us from God, are remitted; and from them also is this peace, whereby we are reconciled to God. (5) Since through grace, once sins are remitted, hostilities dissolve, we now in peace may cling to him from whom our sins alone had torn us. As the prophet says: (6) "He will not weigh down his ears so that he will not hear: rather it is your sins that separate you from God" (Is. 59:1f.). But when these sins have been remitted through faith in our Lord Jesus Christ, we will have peace with no separation intervening between us and God.

9. Perhaps, moreover, someone may wonder how the justice of God the Judge should be understood when God offers grace for the forgiveness of sinners. (2) But clearly God is just in this, for it is truly just that they, who repent their sins before the manifest terror of their penalty appears, are mercifully separated from those who, stubbornly seeking defenses for their sins, do not wish to be corrected by any penitence. (3) For it is unjust that this former group who did not spurn God's call, and who when sinning displeased themselves, be joined in common punishment with that latter group, for just as God hated their sins, so too did they. (4) For this is precisely the discipline of human righteousness: not to love in ourselves anything but what is from God, and to hate what is purely ourselves; nor to approve our own sins nor condemn sins in anyone save ourselves; nor to think it enough to be displeased with our own sins unless in turn we avoid them with the most vigilant effort; nor to think that in avoiding sins our own strength suffices unless we are divinely aided. (5) Therefore God justly forgives such people for whatever they have done before, lest (which would be most unjust) they be mixed in and lumped together with the unrepentant. (6) Wherefore God is just in forgiving such people, and, since he forgives them, he is gracious. Just, then, is the grace of God, and gracious is his justice. And here too grace precedes the reward of repentance, so that no one can repent his own sin unless he is first admonished by God's call.

10. Moreover, so steadfast is divine justice that even though the spiritual and eternal penalty will be relaxed for the man who repents, nevertheless, the bodily afflictions and torments, which we know troubled even the

---

2. Cf. *infra* 12,9–13,6 and n. 3 below.

martyres exercitatos novimus, postremo mors ipsa, quam peccando meruit nostra natura, nulli relaxetur. (2) Quod enim etiam iusti homines et pii tamen exsolvunt ista supplicia, de iusto dei iudicio venire credendum est. (3) Ipsa est quae in sacris scripturis etiam disciplina nominatur, quam nemo iustorum effugere sinitur. (4) Neminem quippe excepit, cum diceret: *Quem enim diligit deus, corripit, flagellat autem omnem filium quem recipit.* Unde etiam ipse Iob, qui propterea tam multa illa passus est, ut hominibus quis vir esset et quantus dei servus eluceret, poenas tamen corporis pro peccatis suis se exsolvere saepe testatur. (5) Petrus quoque apostolus exhortans fratres ad perferendas pro Christi nomine passiones ita loquitur: *Nemo autem vestrum patiatur quasi homicida aut fur aut maledicus aut curas alienas agens; si vero quasi christianus, non erubescat, glorificet autem deum in isto nomine, quia tempus inchoationis iudicii a domo dei. Si autem initium a nobis, quis finis eorum qui non credunt dei evangelio? Et si iustus quidem vix salvus fit, peccator et impius ubi parebit?* (6) Manifeste ostendit easdem ipsas passiones quas iusti patiuntur ad iudicium dei pertinere, quod inchoari dixit ex domo dei, ut inde coniciatur quantae impiis futurae serventur. (7) Unde etiam ipse Paulus ad Thessalonicenses dicit: *Ita ut et nos ipsi de vobis gloriemur in ecclesiis dei, pro vestra patientia et fide in omnibus persecutionibus vestris et pressuris, quas sustinetis in exemplum iusti iudicii dei.* (8) Quod omnino ad illud respicit, quod ait Petrus tempus esse inchoationis iudicii a domo dei, et illud, quod de propheta interposuit: *Et si iustus vix salvus erit, peccator et impius ubi parebit?* (9) Unde mihi videtur etiam illa, quae per Nathan prophetam regi David comminatus est deus, quamquam statim ignoverit poenitenti, propterea tamen accidisse omnia, ut demonstraretur illam veniam spiritualiter datam propter futurum iudicium poenarum quod expectat eos, qui hoc tempore corrigi nolunt. (10) Dicit enim et alibi Petrus: *Propter hoc enim et mortuis evangelizatum est, ut iudicentur quidem secundum hominem in carne, vivant autem secundum deum in spiritu.* (11) Hoc dixi, ut ostenderem, quantum possem et quantum opportunitas praesentis loci scripturarum sinit, non sic accipiendam gratiam et pacem dei, cum dicitur, ut existiment homines a iustitia deum posse discedere. (12) Nam et ipsam pacem cum promitteret dominus, ait: *Haec dixi, ut in me pacem habeatis, in mundo autem pressuram.* Sed tribulationes et molestiae, cum per iustitiam dei redduntur peccatis, bonos et iustos, et quibus iam plus peccata ipsa displicent quam ulla corporis poena, non reflectunt ad peccandum sed ab omni labe penitus purgant. (13) Pax enim perfecta etiam corporis suo tempore roborabitur, si nunc pacem, quam dominus per fidem dare dignatus est, inconcusse spiritus noster atque incommutabiliter teneat.

martyrs, and finally death itself, which our nature has merited by sinning, are relaxed for no one. (2) For since even just and pious men pay these penalties, one must believe that they stem from the just judgments of God. (3) This, which not even one of the just may avoid, the sacred scriptures call discipline. (4) Indeed Paul exempted no one when he said, "He whom God loves, he corrects, and he whips every son whom he receives" (Heb. 12:6). Whence even Job himself, who suffered many torments that he might glowingly exhibit to men what sort of man he was, and his greatness as God's servant, nevertheless often testifies that he suffered bodily penalties on account of his sins. (5) And also Peter the Apostle, exhorting his brethren to endure sufferings for Christ's name, says: "But let none of you suffer as a murderer or a thief or a slanderer or a coveter of other men's goods; but if one suffers as a Christian, let him not be ashamed, but let him glorify God in that name. For the time has come that judgment should begin with God's own house; but if it begins with us, what will be their end who do not believe in the Gospel of God? And if the just man will scarcely be saved, where will the sinner and the impious man appear?" (1 Pet. 4:15-18; cf. Prov. 11:31). (6) Clearly Peter teaches that the sufferings of the just stem from God's judgment, which begins with God's own house, so that one might infer from this what great future sufferings are reserved for the impious. (7) So too Paul himself says to the Thessalonians: "Wherefore even we ourselves glory in you in the churches of God, because of your steadfastness and faith in all your persecutions and afflictions, which you endure as an example of the just judgment of God" (2 Thess. 1:4f.). (8) This completely corresponds both to Peter's statement that it is time for judgment to begin with God's own house, and to the quotation from the prophet that he adduces here: "and if the just man will scarcely be saved, where will the sinner and the impious man appear?" (Prov. 11:31). (9) For this reason also, I think, God threatened King David through his prophet Nathan (2 Sam. 12). Even though God quickly forgave David once he repented, all those calamities nevertheless befell him. This was to show that pardon had been granted spiritually, to warn those who do not wish to be corrected now of what future punishments await them. (10) And Peter says elsewhere: "For this is why the Gospel was preached even to the dead, so that although they were judged in the flesh as men, they might live according to God in the Spirit" (1 Pet. 4:6). (11) I have said this to show, as much as I could and as much as the present passage of scripture permits, that the grace and peace of God should not be so interpreted that men think that God can deviate from justice. (12) For even when the Lord promised his peace, he said, "I have said these things so that you might have peace in me, but affliction in the world" (Jn 16:33). But tribulations and troubles when given through God's justice as retribution for sins do not turn good and just men to sin. Their sins displease them more than any bodily pain, and these trials and tribulations purge them completely of every stain. (13) For the perfect peace of the body will be confirmed in due time, if now our spirit holds unshakeably and unchangingly to the peace which the Lord has deigned to give us through faith.

11. Quod autem apostolus gratiam et pacem a deo patre et domino nostro Iesu Christo dicit non adiungens etiam spiritum sanctum, non mihi alia ratio videtur nisi quia ipsum donum dei spiritum sanctum intelligimus. Gratia porro et pax quid aliud quam donum dei? (2) Unde nullo modo dari hominibus gratia potest, qua liberamur a peccatis, et pax, qua reconciliamur deo, nisi in spiritu sancto. Et ideo ipsa trinitas pariterque incommutabilis unitas in ista salutatione cognoscitur. (3) Quod propterea maxime credo, quoniam excepta epistola, quam ad Hebraeos scripsit, ubi principium salutatorium de industria dicitur omisisse, ne Iudaei, qui adversus eum pugnaciter oblatrabant, nomine eius offensi vel inimico animo legerent vel omnino legere non curarent quod ad eorum salutem scripserat; (4) unde nonnulli eam in canonem scripturarum recipere timuerunt—sed quoquo modo se habeat ista quaestio, excepta hac epistola ceterae omnes, quae nulla dubitante ecclesia Pauli apostoli esse firmantur, talem continent salutationem, nisi quod ad Timotheum in utraque interponit misericordiam. (5) Nam ita scribit: *Gratia, misericordia, pax a deo patre et Iesu Christo domino nostro.* (6) Quo enim familiarius eo dulcius quodammodo scribens ad Timotheum id verbum interposuit, quo plane aperitur atque ostenditur non meritis operum priorum sed secundum misericordiam dei nobis dari spiritum sanctum, ut et peccatorum abolitio fiat, quibus seiungebamur a deo, et reconciliatio, ut illi inhaereamus.

12. Nec aliae apostolorum epistolae, quas usus ecclesiasticus recipit, parum nos admonent de ista trinitate in principiis suis. (2) Nam Petrus ita dicit: *Gratia vobis et pax adimpleatur,* deinde statim subicit: *Benedictus deus et pater domini nostri Iesu Christi,* ut per gratiam et pacem spiritu sancto intellecto patris et filii commemoratio animum de trinitate commoneat. (3) Et in alia sic ait: *Gratia vobis et pax multiplicetur in recognitione dei et Christi Iesu domini nostri.* (4) Iohannes autem nescio quam ob causam omisit tale principium, sed plane trinitatis commemorationem nec ipse neglexit pro gratia et pace societatem interponens: *Quod ergo vidimus,* inquit, *nuntiamus et vobis, ut et vos societatem habeatis nobiscum et societas nostra sit cum patre et filio eius Iesu Christo.* (5) In secunda vero illis, quae ad Timotheum sunt, consonat dicens: *Sit vobiscum gratia, misericordia, pax a deo patre et Iesu Christo filio patris.* (6) In tertiae principio de trinitate penitus tacetur, credo, quod sit omnino brevissima. Sic enim incipit: *Senior Gaio dilectissimo, quem ego diligo in veritate.* Quam veritatem pro ipsa trinitate positam puto. (7) Iudas nominato deo patre et domino Iesu Christo ad intelligendum spiritum sanctum, hoc est donum dei, tria verba ponit.

11. The Apostle says "Grace and peace from God our Father and our Lord Jesus Christ" without adding the Holy Spirit. He does this explicitly, it seems to me, so we might understand that this very gift of God is precisely the Holy Spirit. Indeed, are grace and peace anything other than God's gift? (2) For grace, which frees us from sin, and peace, which reconciles us to God, are given to men only through the Holy Spirit. And thus this salutation equally acknowledges the Trinity and also the unchangeable divine unity. (3) I believe this absolutely because Paul habitually begins his letters with this salutation, with the exception of his letter to the Hebrews. There he omits it intentionally lest the Jews, who were belligerently railing against him, be offended by this name and so either read with hostile spirit or choose not to read at all what he had written for their salvation. (4) Some people hesitated to receive this letter into the canon for this reason. But be that as it may, with this one exception, all the other letters universally affirmed by the churches to be Paul's contain such a salutation, except where Paul in his two letters to Timothy interposes the word "mercy." (5) There he writes: "Grace, mercy, and peace from God the Father and Jesus Christ our Lord." (6) He does this since he writes to Timothy in a manner more familiar and hence somewhat sweeter. And by this word he clearly explained and taught that the Holy Spirit is granted to us not because of the merits of our earlier works, but through God's mercy, in order to accomplish both the abolition of our sins, which had separated us from God, and our reconciliation, that we might cling to him.

12. Nor does any other ecclesiastically accepted apostolic letter speak to us insufficiently of the Trinity in its opening lines. (2) For Peter says: "May grace and peace be multiplied among you," and then immediately adds, "Blessed be the God and Father of our Lord Jesus Christ" (1 Pet. 1:2–3), so that, since grace and peace indicate the Holy Spirit, his calling to mind the Father and Son reminds us of the Trinity. (3) Accordingly he says in his other letter: "May grace and peace be multiplied among you in the knowledge of God and Christ Jesus our Lord" (2 Pet. 1:2). (4) John also, for some reason or other, omitted such a beginning, but clearly he did not neglect to call to mind the Trinity, using "fellowship" in the place of "grace" and "peace": "That which we have seen," he says, "we announce also to you, both so you might have fellowship with us, and so our fellowship might be with the Father and his son Jesus Christ" (1 Jn. 1:3). (5) But in his second letter, John repeats what Paul had said to Timothy: "May grace be with you, and mercy, and peace from God the Father and Jesus Christ the Son of the Father" (2 Jn. 1:3). (6) In the beginning of the third letter, John is completely silent about the Trinity, I think, because the letter is so very brief. For he begins thus: "The Elder to the most beloved Gaius, whom I love in truth" (3 Jn. 1:1); but "truth" here, I think, stands for the Trinity. (7) Jude, having named God the Father and the Lord Jesus Christ, then uses three words by which one understands the Holy Spirit (which is the gift of God):

Sic quippe incipit: *Iudas Iesu Christi servus, frater autem Iacobi, in deo patre dilectis et Iesu Christo conservatis, vocatis, misericordia vobis et pax et caritas adimpleatur.* (8) Gratia enim et pax sine misericordia et caritate intelligi non potest. Iacobus autem usitatissimum exordium fecit epi-
5 stolae ita scribens: *Iacobus dei et domini nostri Iesu Christi servus duodecim tribubus, quae sunt in dispersione, salutem,* (9) credo, considerans salutem non esse nisi in dono dei, ubi gratia et pax. Et quamquam ante hoc verbum nominaverit deum et dominum nostrum Iesum Christum, tamen quia nulla gratia et nulla pace salvi fiunt homines nisi quae
10 est a deo patre et domino Iesu Christo, sicut Iohannes in tertia veritatem, sic iste salutem pro ipsa trinitate posuisse mihi videtur.

13. Quo loco prorsus non arbitror praetereundum, quod pater Valerius animadvertit admirans in quorundam rusticanorum collocutione. Cum alter alteri dixisset: *salus,* quaesivit ab eo qui et Latine nos-
15 set et Punice, quid esset *salus;* responsum est: *tria.* (2) Tum ille agnoscens cum gaudio salutem nostram esse trinitatem concinentia linguarum non fortuitu sic sonuisse arbitratus est, sed occultissima dispensatione divinae providentiae, ut, cum latine nominatur *salus,* a Punicis intelligantur *tria,* et, cum Punici lingua sua *tria* nominant,
20 Latine intelligatur *salus.* (3) Chananaea enim, hoc est Punica mulier de finibus Tyri et Sidonis egressa, quae in evangelio personam gentium gerit, salutem petebat filiae suae, cui responsum est a domino: *Non est bonum panem filiorum mittere canibus.* (4) Quod crimen obiectum illa non negans tamquam de confessione peccatorum impetratura salutem
25 filiae, hoc est novae vitae suae: *Ita,* inquit, *domine. Nam et canes edunt de micis quae cadunt de mensa dominorum suorum.* (5) Tria enim mulieris lingua salus vocantur: erat enim Chananaea. Unde interrogati rustici nostri, quid sint, Punice respondentes: Chanani, corrupta scilicet, sicut in talibus solet, una littera, quid aliud respondent
30 quam: Chananaei? (6) Petens itaque salutem trinitatem petebat, quia et Romana lingua, quae in salutis nomine trinitatem Punice sonat, caput gentium inventa est in adventu domini; et diximus Chananaeam mulierem gentium sustinere personam. Panem autem appellans dominus id ipsum, quod a muliere petebatur, quid aliud quam trinitati
35 attestatur? (7) Namque alio loco eandem trinitatem

"Jude the servant of Jesus Christ, brother of James, to those who are beloved in God the Father and preserved for Jesus Christ and called; may mercy and peace and love be multiplied among you" (Jude 1:1-2), (8) for one cannot understand grace and peace without mercy and love. Furthermore, James opened his letter with a most familiar beginning, writing: "James the servant of God and our Lord Jesus Christ to the twelve tribes of diaspora, greetings" (Jms. 1:1), (9) thinking, I believe, that greetings[3] can exist only through the gift of God, wherein is also grace and peace. And even though before this word, "greetings," he had named God and our Lord Jesus Christ, nonetheless, since men are saved only by the grace and peace of God the Father and the Lord Jesus Christ, it seems to me that, just as John used "truth" in his third letter, so James has used this word "greetings" here to stand for the Trinity.

13. I certainly do not think I should neglect to mention here something that Father Valerius[4] noticed with amazement in the conversation of certain peasants [which was in Punic]. Overhearing one say "salus" to the other, Valerius asked the one who knew both Latin and Punic what "salus" meant. The peasant answered, "Three." (2) Then Valerius, realizing with joy that our word for greeting, "salus," means "trinity," thought that this harmony of languages was no accident, but rather the most hidden dispensation of divine providence. For when one says "salus" in Latin, a Carthaginian understands it as "three"; and when Carthaginians say "three" in their own language, it is understood in Latin as "salvation." (3) Furthermore, when the Canaanite woman (that is, the Punic or Phoenician woman from the region of Tyre and Sidon who represents the Gentiles in the Gospel) petitioned for her daughter's health, the Lord answered her: "It is not fitting to throw the children's bread to dogs" (Mt 15:26). (4) She accepted this humiliation as if by the confession of sins she was about to obtain health [or "salvation"] for her daughter, that is, her new life. "Yes, Lord," she said, "but even dogs eat the crumbs which fall from their lords' table" (Mt 15:27). (5) Now in this Canaanite woman's tongue, "three" sounds like "salus"—for if you ask our peasants what they are, they will answer in Punic "Chanani" which, although it is missing a letter, which is usual in such cases, can mean nothing other than "Canaanite." (6) And so in asking for health the woman asked for the Trinity, for the Roman word, which names "trinity" in Punic, is the noun for "salvation." And so the woman turned out to be the first of the Gentiles at the Lord's coming, for we have said that she represents the Gentiles. Moreover, when the Lord responded as if the woman had asked for bread, to what did he witness, if not the Trinity?—(7) for he clearly teaches elsewhere that one might think of the Trinity itself as

---
3. *Salus*—"greetings," "salvation," "health." Augustine exploits all these meanings to make his argument through 13,6. Where a passage depends on all these multiple meanings, I have left "salus" in the text.

4. The bishop of Hippo while Augustine was presbyter and later co-adjutor bishop.

in tribus panibus intelligendam esse apertissime docet. Sed haec verborum consonantia sive provenerit sive provisa sit, non pugnaciter agendum est ut ei quisque consentiat, sed quantum interpretantis elegantiam hilaritas audientis admittit.

5 **14.** Illud sane magna intentione animi considerandum et totis viribus pietatis amplectendum satis apparet, quoniam, si gratia et pax ad implendam trinitatis commemorationem sic ab apostolo ponitur, ac si sanctum spiritum nominet, ille peccat in spiritum sanctum qui desperans vel irridens atque contemnens praedicationem gratiae, per
10 quam peccata diluuntur, et pacis, per quam reconciliamur deo, detrectat agere poenitentiam de peccatis suis et in eorum impia atque mortifera quadam suavitate perdurandum sibi esse decernit et in finem usque perdurat. (2) Quod ergo ait dominus dimitti homini, si verbum dixerit adversus filium hominis; si autem verbum dixerit adversus spiritum
15 sanctum, non ei dimitti neque hic neque in futuro saeculo, sed reum esse aeterni peccati, non negligenter audiendum est. (3) Constituamus enim aliquem Latinae linguae ignarum, cum illo audiente pronuntiatus fuerit ab aliquo spiritus sanctus, quaerentem quid rerum significetur sub isto syllabarum sono; ab aliquo autem deceptore vel irrisore impio
20 responderi aliquid aliud, quodlibet vile et abiectum, ut quaerentem decipiat, sicuti a talibus fieri solet ridendi gratia; illum autem per ignorantiam contempsisse hoc nomen, dum nescit quid significet, et aliqua etiam in hoc convicia iactitasse: neminem esse arbitror tam vanum et inconsideratum, qui hunc hominem ullo crimine impietatis aspergat.
25 (4) At contra si tacito nomine res ipsa verbis, quibus potest, ad quaerentis intelligentiam perducatur, tum vero, si aliqua contumeliose in tantam sanctitatem vel verba vel facta protulerit, reus tenebitur. (5) Quae cum ita sint, manifestum esse arbitror eum, qui hoc nomine audito aliam pro alia rem significari putaverit et adversus eam rem,
30 quam significari hoc nomine credidit, verbum dixerit, non hunc sic peccare ut adversus spiritum sanctum verbum dixisse iudicetur. (6) Itaque si quisquam quaerens, quid sit spiritus sanctus, audiat ab imperito hunc esse filium dei, per quem facta sunt omnia, qui etiam certa opportunitate temporis de virgine natus sit et occisus a Iudaeis et resurrexerit,
35 quibus auditis vel neget vel irrideat quae dicta sunt, non eum sic teneri putandum est ac si verbum adversus spiritum sanctum dixerit, sed potius adversus filium dei vel filium hominis, sicut et vocari et esse dignatus est. (7) Non enim, quid sit imperito per vocem propositum, sed per rationem expositum, considerandum est, quia ille, cum maledicta
40 proferret, ei utique maledicebat quem sibi enarratum cogitatione intuebatur. Quodlibet autem vocaretur, utrum res ipsa veneranda an neganda vel vituperanda esset, hoc quaeritur. (8) Hoc modo etiam si quispiam quaerat quid sit Iesus Christus,

three loaves of bread (cf. Lk 11:5-13). But whether this consonance of words came about by accident or by Providence should not be pursued aggressively with a view to winning full agreement, but enough so that the pleasure of the listener might make allowance for the finesse of the interpreter.

14. Clearly then one should consider this with great mental rigor and embrace it with all the strength of piety: that is, if Paul uses "grace" and "peace" to stand for the Holy Spirit in his invocation of the Trinity, then the person who despairs of or ridicules or belittles the prediction of grace, which washes away sins, and peace, which reconciles us to God, and who then refuses to repent for his sins, sins against the Holy Spirit. For thus he decides that he must continue in sin's impiety and death-bringing sweetness, and so he continues to the end. (2) The Lord therefore said that a man would be forgiven if he spoke a word against the Son of Man, but that if he spoke against the Holy Spirit, he would be forgiven neither in this world nor in the next, but would be guilty of eternal sin, because this sin would not be heard lightly (Mt 12:31f). (3) Let us suppose that someone did not know Latin and, hearing someone else pronounce the words "Holy Spirit," that he asked another person what these syllables signified. And let us suppose that this other person was a liar or an impious joker, and that he told him something other than the truth, something vile and lowly to deceive the questioner, as this sort of person will usually do for a joke. And let us suppose that this first man, through ignorance, was contemptuous of the name of the Holy Spirit, not knowing what it signified, and furthermore, that he hurled some insults against it. No one, I think, would be so vacuous and unthinking as to accuse this man of any crime of impiety. (4) On the other hand, if somebody explained to the questioner by whatever means not the name of the Holy Spirit but the idea of it itself, and still he proceeded to speak or act abusively against such sanctity, he would then be considered guilty. (5) Thus I consider it obvious that if someone hearing the name of the Holy Spirit thinks that it signifies something else entirely, and speaks against what he took the name to signify, he would not thereby be held to have sinned by speaking against the Holy Spirit. (6) So too, if anyone asks what the Holy Spirit is, and hears from some ignorant person that it is the Son of God through whom all things were made, and who at the appointed hour was born of a virgin, killed by the Jews, and then raised, and then having heard these things the person denies or mocks what he had heard, he should not be judged to have spoken against the Holy Spirit. Rather, he spoke against the Son of God or of Man, as Jesus Christ deigned to be called and to be. (7) For one ought to consider not what the questioner's voice said, but what his reason set forth, since that man when he blasphemed certainly maligned the Son of God or Man, though he thought it the Holy Spirit who had been reported to him. For the true question here is not what the concept is called, but whether it was itself actually venerated or denied and cursed. (8) Likewise if anyone asks what Jesus

et ea quaerenti respondeantur quae non in filium dei sed potius in spiritum sanctum conveniunt, quibus auditis ille blasphemet, non utique adversus filium, sed adversus spiritum sanctum verbum dixisse tenebitur.

15. Sed si transitorie ac negligenter attenderimus quod dictum est: *Si quis verbum dixerit adversus spiritum sanctum, non remittetur ei neque in hoc saeculo neque in futuro,* quis inveniri poterit, cui veniam peccatorum dederit deus? (2) Nam et pagani qui appellantur, etiam nunc totam nostram religionem, quia iam ferro et caedibus prohibentur, maledictis contumeliisque insectantur et, quicquid de ipsa trinitate dicimus, negando et blasphemando contemnunt. (3) Non enim excipiunt sibi spiritum sanctum, quem venerentur, ut in cetera saeviant, sed simul adversus omnia, quaecumque sollicite de trina dei maiestate loquimur, quanto possunt furore impietatis, oblatrant. Nam neque de ipso deo patre digne sentiunt, quem partim penitus negant, partim sic fatentur, ut de illo falsa fingendo non utique illum sed sua figmenta venerentur. (4) Multo magis ergo, quod de filio dei vel de spiritu sancto dicimus, suo impio more deridere quam nostra pia societate colere maluerunt. Quos tamen quantum possumus adhortamur ad Christum cognoscendum et per ipsum patrem deum summoque et vero imperatori militandum esse suademus eosque promissa impunitate praeteritorum omnium peccatorum invitamus ad fidem. (5) Qua in re satis iudicamus, etiam si quid adversus spiritum sanctum in sua sacrilega superstitione dixerunt, cum christiani facti fuerint, sine ulla caligine dubitationis ignosci. Iudaei vero quales adversus spiritum sanctum fuerint, testis est Stephanus, quem ipso spiritu sancto plenum lapidaverunt, cum illa omnia quae in eos dixit, ipse spiritus dixerit. (6) In quibus verbis apertissime dictum est Iudaeis: *Vos semper restitistis spiritui sancto.* In illo tamen numero Iudaeorum resistentium spiritui sancto et non ob aliud Stephanum vas eius, nisi quod eo plenus erat, lapidantium etiam Paulus apostolus erat in manibus omnium, quorum vestimenta servabat; quod sibi postea etiam poenitendo increpitat eo ipso spiritu iam plenissimus, cui primo inanissimus resistebat, et paratus iam lapidari pro talibus dictis, qualium praedicatorem ipse lapidaverat. (7) Quid Samaritani? Nonne ita spiritui sancto adversantur ut ipsam prophetiam penitus conentur extinguere, quae per spiritum sanctum ministrata est? (8) Quorum tamen saluti et ipse dominus attestatur in eo, qui de leprosis decem mundatis solus reversus est ut ageret gratias, cum esset Samaritanus, et in illa muliere, cum qua ad puteum sexta hora locutus est, et

Christ is and receives an answer which applies not to the Son of God but rather to the Holy Spirit, and then the questioner blasphemes against what he heard, he certainly does not speak against the Son, but rather against the Holy Spirit.

15. If we attend cursorily or carelessly to this statement, "If anyone speaks a word against the Holy Spirit, he will not be forgiven either in this world or in the one to come" (Mt 12:32), who could be found whom God could pardon for his sins? (2) For even now those who are called pagans attack our entire religion, no longer with sword and slaughter, since they are prohibited from doing so, but with curses and insults, and they scorn with denials and blasphemy whatever we say about the Trinity itself. (3) They make no exception of the Holy Spirit, that they might worship it and so concentrate their violence on the other two members of the Trinity, but rather they snarl with the greatest fury and impiety possible against any statement of the triple majesty of God that we might cautiously offer. Nor do they consider with fitting respect God the Father himself, for some deny him entirely, while others imagine such false things about him that they end by worshipping not him but their own inventions. (4) They impiously ridicule what we say about the Son of God or the Holy Spirit that much more, preferring ridicule to worship in pious association with us. Nonetheless we urge them as much as we can to acknowledge Christ and through him God the Father; we urge them to fight for the true, the highest Emperor; and we invite them with the promise of pardon for all their past sins to join the faith. (5) For in this matter we consider that even if they in their sacrilegious superstition had spoken against the Holy Spirit, once they become Christians, they are pardoned beyond any shadow of a doubt. As for Jewish hostility to the Holy Spirit, Stephen himself is a witness. For they stoned him when he was full of the Holy Spirit, because he said to them the same things the Spirit had once said (Acts 6:8–7:60). (6) And he most clearly told the Jews: "You have always resisted the Holy Spirit" (Acts 7:51). But nonetheless among those Jews resisting the Holy Spirit and stoning Stephen its vessel precisely because he was filled with this same Spirit was Paul the Apostle, who held all their garments. He later reproached himself regretfully for that incident when he himself was filled with that same Spirit which he at first had foolishly resisted. And he was prepared to be stoned for saying the same sort of things for which he had stoned the preacher, Stephen. (7) And what of the Samaritans? Do not they too oppose the Holy Spirit to the extent that they try to extinguish completely that prophecy mediated through it?[5] (8) Nonetheless the Lord himself confirms their salvation by various examples: that man from among the ten cleansed lepers who alone returned to give thanks, though he was a Samaritan (Lk 17:15f.); and the woman at the well whom he spoke with at the sixth hour (Jn 4:7); and

---

5. The Samaritans reject the prophets in that they accept only the Pentateuch as authentic scripture.

eis, qui per illam crediderunt. (9) Post domini autem ascensionem, sicut in Actibus Apostolorum scriptum est, quanta gratulatione sanctorum recepit Samaria verbum dei? (10) Simonem quoque magum arguens Petrus apostolus, quod tam male de spiritu sancto senserit, ut
5 eum venalem putans pecunia sibi emendum poposcerit, non tamen ita de illo desperavit ut veniae locum nullum relinqueret. Nam benigne etiam, ut eum poeniteret, admonuit. (11) Ipsa denique catholicae ecclesiae tam insignis auctoritas, quae in eodem dono spiritus sancti omnium sanctorum mater toto fecunda orbe diffunditur, cui umquam
10 haeretico vel scismatico spem liberationis, si se corrigat, amputavit? (12) cui placandi dei aditum clausit? Nonne omnes ad ubera sua, quae superbo fastidio reliquerunt, cum lacrimis revocat? Quis vero vel de principibus vel de gregibus haereticorum invenitur, qui non adversetur spiritui sancto? Nisi forte quisquam tam perverse sentit, ut arbitretur
15 eum teneri reum, qui adversus spiritum sanctum aliquid dixerit, eum vero, qui adversus spiritum sanctum multa fecerit, non teneri. (13) Qui autem tanta evidentia contra spiritum sanctum pugnant quam illi qui adversus ecclesiae pacem superbissimis contentionibus saeviunt? Sed si de verbis quaestio est, quaero utrum nihil dicant adversus spiri-
20 tum sanctum, cum alii eum, quod ad ipsum proprie pertinet, omnino non esse asseverent, sed ita esse unum deum ut idem ipse pater, idem ipse filius, idem ipse spiritus sanctus appelletur; (14) alii fateantur quidem esse spiritum sanctum, sed aequalem filio vel omnino esse deum negent; alii unam quidem et eandem trinitatis substantiam esse
25 fateantur, sed de ipsa divina substantia tam impie sentiant ut eam commutabilem et corruptibilem putent, ipsumque spiritum sanctum, quem dominus discipulis se missurum esse promisit, non quinquagesimo die post eius resurrectionem, sicut Apostolorum Acta testantur, sed post trecentos fere annos per hominem venisse confingant; (15) alii similiter
30 adventum eius, quem tenemus, negent et eum prophetas in Phrygia, per quos tanto post loqueretur, elegisse contendant; alii sacramenta eius exsufflent et baptizatos in nomine patris et filii et spiritus sancti denuo baptizare non dubitent. (16) Sed ne pergam per singula, quae sunt innumerabilia, his certe omnibus, quos pro tempore breviter attigi,
35 ad sponsam Christi redeuntibus et errorem atque impietatem poenitendo damnantibus nulla catholica disciplina negandam ecclesiae pacem et claudenda viscera misericordiae iudicavit.

16. Quod si quisquam tunc putat verbum dici adversus spiritum sanctum, cum ab eo dicitur, cui iam per baptismum dimissa peccata
40 sunt,

those who believed because of her (Jn 4:42). (9) Moreover, after the Lord's ascension, does not the *Acts of the Apostles* relate the great joy on the part of the saints at Samaria's reception of the word of God (Acts 8:9)? (10) Also the apostle Peter charged Simon Magus, because Simon had held the Spirit in such low esteem that he thought it was for sale and demanded it with money. But Peter did not so despair of Simon that he left no place for forgiveness; rather, he benignly admonished him to repent (Acts 8:9-22). (11) And finally that great authority of the Catholic Church, the mother of all the saints by that same gift of the Holy Spirit, spread with such fecundity throughout the whole world—to what heretic or schismatic has she ever cut off the hope of salvation, if he correct himself? (12) To whom has she shut off access to placating God? Does she not with tears call back to her breast all who in proud haughtiness have left her? But what heretic, be he leader or follower, does not oppose the Holy Spirit? Or is anyone so perverse as to think that only he who speaks against the Holy Spirit, and not he who does many things against it, should be considered guilty? (13) For who more clearly fights against the Holy Spirit than those whose arrogant arguments rage against the peace of the Church? But if it is a question of words, I ask whether nothing is said against the Holy Spirit when some, denying that the Spirit's proper and specific offices exist at all, maintain that God is One, and is only variously labeled the Father or the Son or the Holy Spirit?[6] (14) Others acknowledge the Spirit's existence but deny its equality to the Son, or that it is God at all.[7] Others acknowledge the Trinity's single nature and essence, but they think so impiously as to consider this divine nature changeable and subject to corruption. Further, they pretend that this very same Holy Spirit, which the Lord had promised to send to his disciples, had come not on the fiftieth day after the Lord's resurrection, as the *Acts of the Apostles* testifies (Acts 2:1-4), but only after some three hundred years in the form of a man.[8] (15) Others similarly deny the coming of the Spirit that we hold, and contend that it elected prophets in Phrygia, through whom the Spirit spoke so much afterwards.[9] Others blow away the Spirit's sacraments and do not hesitate to baptize again those already baptized in the name of the Father and of the Son and of the Holy Spirit.[10] (16) I will not continue through this endless list. But surely, when all these (whom for time's sake I have touched on only briefly) return to the Bride of Christ and condemn by repentance their error and impiety, no Catholic teaching holds that they will be denied the peace of the Church, nor will the bowels of mercy be closed to them.

16. But if anyone then concludes from this that someone whose sins have already been remitted through baptism is the one who speaks

---

6. Modalists. This begins a catena of anti-heretical remarks.
7. Subordinationists.
8. Manichees
9. Montanists.
10. Donatists.

attendat nec talibus per ecclesiae sanctitatem auferri poenitentiae locum. (2) Si enim propterea credit non dari veniam, quia gratia fidei sacramentisque fidelium iam perceptis non potest dici peccasse ignorantia, videat aliam causam esse, cum dicitur propterea non ignosci, quia non ignorantiae tempore peccatum est, et aliam causam esse, cum dicitur propterea non ignosci, quia verbum dixit adversus spiritum sanctum. (3) Si enim sola ignorantia veniam meretur et ignorantia non accipitur nisi antequam quisque fuerit baptizatus, non solum si adversus spiritum sanctum, sed etiam si adversus filium hominis post baptismum dixerit verbum, et omnino si qua fornicatione vel homicidio vel ullo flagitio aut facinore post baptismum sese maculaverit, non potest poenitendo curari. (4) Quod qui senserunt, exclusi sunt a communione catholica satisque iudicatum est eos in illa crudelitate divinae misericordiae participes esse non posse. (5) Si autem illud solum, quod adversus spiritum sanctum dicitur, sine venia esse post acceptum baptismum putatur, primo dominus, cum inde loqueretur, nullum tempus excepit sed regulariter ait: *Qui dixerit verbum adversus spiritum sanctum non remittetur ei neque in hoc saeculo neque in futuro.* (6) Deinde Simon, quem paulo ante commemoravi, iam baptismum acceperat, cum spiritum sanctum turpissimo mercatui subditum credidit, cui correpto a se Petrus tamen consilium poenitendi dedit. (7) Quid autem de his qui cum baptismi sacramenta pueri vel etiam infantes perceperint, postea negligenter educati per ignorantiae tenebras vitam turpissimam ducant nescientes omnino, quid christiana disciplina iubeat aut vetet, quid polliceatur et quid minetur, quid credendum, quid sperandum, quid diligendum sit; (8) num audebimus peccata eorum propterea non ignorantiae peccata deputare, quia baptizati peccaverunt, cum omnino ignorantes et omnino, quemadmodum dicitur, ubi caput haberent, nescientes in magno errore peccaverint?

17. Quod si eo tempore cum scientia quisque peccasse dicatur, quo scit malum esse quod facit et tamen facit, cur hoc in spiritum sanctum solum, non etiam in dominum Iesum Christum irremissibile iudicatur? (2) Aut si hoc ipsum esse creditur peccare vel verbum dicere adversus spiritum sanctum, quodlibet peccatum cum scientia committere, ut, quicquid homines ignorando peccant, in filium peccare, quicquid autem scientes peccant, in spiritum sanctum peccare iudicentur, quaero quis nesciat malum esse verbi gratia corrumpere pudicitiam uxoris alienae, vel eo ipso certe, quod hoc in sua coniuge nollet perpeti, aut fraudare quemquam in negotio aut circumvenire mendacio aut opprimere testimonii falsitate aut auferendae rei eius causa insidiari et occidere quempiam, et si quid omnino est, quod sibi ab altero fieri non vult, et si fieri senserit, toto corde indubitanter accusat? (3) Aut si haec ab ignorantibus fieri dicimus, quid inveniemus in quo scientes homines peccare videantur? (4) Restat ergo ut, si hoc est peccare in

unforgivably against the Holy Spirit, let him mark that such people have never been denied the opportunity to repent such things through the holiness of the Church. (2) For if one therefore thinks that forgiveness is denied because such a person, already in the Church through the grace of faith and the reception of the sacraments, cannot be said to have sinned through ignorance, let him see that these are two different considerations: forgiveness for a sin committed knowingly and not from ignorance, and forgiveness for having spoken against the Holy Spirit. (3) For if ignorance alone merits pardon, and ignorance is admissable only prior to baptism, then no baptized person having spoken against the Holy Spirit or the Son of Man, or having stained himself by fornication or homicide or any other offense or crime after baptism, could be healed after repenting. (4) Those maintaining this opinion have been excluded from the Catholic communion, and rightly has their own harshness denied them participation in divine mercy.[11] (5) Why say that after baptism the word spoken against the Holy Spirit cannot be forgiven? For in the first place, when the Lord taught this, he set no time limits but simply said: "Who has spoken a word against the Holy Spirit will not be forgiven either in this world or in the one to come." (6) But Simon Magus, whom I mentioned a little earlier, had already received baptism when he believed that the Holy Spirit was subject to most foul traffic; and nonetheless Peter, after correcting him, counseled repentance. (7) Finally, what about those who, though baptized in childhood or infancy, nevertheless later on, negligently educated, lead the most disgraceful lives in the darkness of ignorance, utterly unacquainted with Christian commandments and prohibitions, with what is promised and what threatened, with what ought to be believed and hoped for and loved? (8) Will we dare consider their sins not sins of ignorance simply because they sinned after baptism when, completely ignorant, not even knowing, as the saying goes, where their own head is, they have sinned in great error?

17. But if someone knowingly sins, conscious that what he does is bad and yet doing it, why consider this unforgivable only if it is directed against the Holy Spirit, and not against the Lord Jesus Christ? (2) Or is the sin committed knowingly like a word spoken against the Holy Spirit, so that the various sins of ignorance are sins against the Son, but sins committed knowingly are sins against the Holy Spirit? But, I ask, who does not think that corrupting the chastity of another's wife is evil, if for no other reason than that he would not wish to endure this with his own wife? Who does not know that deceit in a business deal, or mendacity, or oppression by false testimony, or stealing property through treachery and murder, is evil? Who, if anyone does something to him that he does not want done to himself, hesitates to accuse this person with his whole heart? (3) Can we say that such things are sins of ignorance? What sin, then, could a man possibly do knowingly? (4) It follows therefore that these are sins against the Holy

---

11. Novationists.

spiritum sanctum peccare cum scientia, illis peccatis quae commemoravi negetur poenitendi locus, quoniam peccato in spiritum sanctum omnem spem veniae dominus amputavit. Quod si regula christiana respuit omnesque illos qui sic peccant ad correctionem vitae vocare non cessat, (5) adhuc quaerendum est quid sit peccare in spiritum sanctum cui peccato venia nulla conceditur.

18. An forte non est dicendus cum scientia peccare, qui peccatum ipsum malum esse novit, et tamen deum voluntatemque eius ignorans peccat. (2) Quod enim videtur et ad Hebraeos dicere, cum dicit: *Voluntarie enim peccantibus nobis postquam accepimus scientiam veritatis, non adhuc relinquitur pro peccatis sacrificium.* (3) Parum enim erat si tantummodo diceret: *Voluntarie peccantibus nobis,* nisi adderet: *postquam accepimus scientiam veritatis,* in qua utique deus voluntasque eius cognoscitur. (4) Quae sententia videtur congruere dominicae illi sententiae, cum ait: *Servus ignorans voluntatem domini sui et faciens digna plagis vapulabit pauca; servus autem sciens voluntatem domini sui et faciens digna plagis vapulabit multa,* (5) ut hoc putemus dictum esse, quod dictum est: *vapulabit pauca,* tamquam si diceret, leviter emendatus ad veniam pertinebit; in eo vero quod dictum est: *vapulabit multa,* sempiternum supplicium intelligatur, quod minatur peccantibus in spiritum sanctum, quibus dicit numquam posse dimitti peccatum, ut hoc sit peccare in spiritum sanctum cognita dei voluntate peccare. (6) Quod si ita est, cogitari oportet et discuti prius, quando cognoscatur voluntas dei. (7) Nonnulli enim et ante perceptum baptismi sacramentum cognoverunt eam. Nam et Cornelius centurio voluntatem dei utique apostolo Petro docente cognovit et ipsum spiritum sanctum manifestissimis coattestantibus signis antequam baptizaretur accepit, quamquam non ideo sacramenta illa contempserit, sed multo certius baptizatus sit, ut etiam ipsa sacrosancta signacula, quorum res in eo praecesserat, ad perficiendam scientiam veritatis percipere nullo modo moraretur. (8) Multi autem nec post acceptum baptismum curant cognoscere voluntatem dei. Quapropter quisquis ante baptismum cognita dei voluntate peccaverit, non possumus dicere aut ullo modo credere, cum ad baptismum accesserit, non ei dimitti omnia quaecumque peccavit. (9) Huc accedit quod, cum voluntas dei in diligendo deo et proximo breviter insinuetur credentibus, ita ut in his duobus praeceptis tota lex pendeat et omnes prophetae—dilectionem autem proximi, id est, (10) dilectionem hominis usque ad inimici dilectionem nobis dominus ipse commendat (11) et videmus, quam multi iam baptizati et vera esse ista fateantur et tamquam domini praecepta venerentur—cum autem perpessi fuerint alicuius inimicitias, ita rapiuntur animo ad ulciscendum et tantis inardescunt facibus odiorum, ut nec prolato et recitato evangelio

Spirit, namely, sins knowingly committed. And the opportunity to repent for these sins which I have just mentioned would be denied, since the Lord cut off all hope of pardon for a sin against the Holy Spirit. But if the Christian rule rejects this view, and unceasingly calls to correction those who so sin, (5) we must then still ask: what is the sin against the Holy Spirit for which no pardon is granted?

18. Or perhaps someone who knows that sin itself is bad, but who goes ahead anyway since he does not know God and God's will, should not be said to sin knowingly? (2) Paul himself seems to say this to the Hebrews when he writes: "For if we sin deliberately after we have received the knowledge of truth, there no longer remains a sacrifice for sins" (Heb. 10:26). (3) It would have been insufficient had he said "If we sin deliberately," without adding, "after we have received knowledge of the truth," which certainly makes known God and his will. (4) And this seems to accord with the Lord's statement: "The servant not knowing his lord's will and doing what deserves punishment will be flogged lightly; but the servant knowing the will of his lord and still doing things deserving punishment will be flogged severely" (Lk 12:47-48). (5) Thus we might take "he will be flogged lightly" as "he will be lightly corrected and will attain pardon," but "he will be flogged severely" as the eternal punishment that threatens those sinning against the Holy Spirit, whose sin Christ says can never be excused. By this interpretation, to sin against the Holy Spirit would mean to sin after knowing the will of God. (6) To maintain this position we must first consider and discuss the question, when is the will of God known? (7) For some have known God's will even before receiving the sacrament of baptism. Cornelius the centurion, for example, both certainly knew the will of God through the apostle Peter's teaching and received the Holy Spirit, as the most manifest signs attested, before he was baptized. All this notwithstanding, however, he did not scorn the sacraments, but rather that much more surely was he baptized. For even though the reality to which these holy marks point had already preceded his baptism, he still hastened to receive them in order to perfect his knowledge of the truth (Acts 10). (8) On the other hand, many people even after receiving baptism do not take care to know God's will. And this is why we can neither say nor by any means believe, if anyone before baptism knew the will of God and still sinned, that he is not forgiven all his sins no matter what they were once he receives the sacrament. (9) We hold this all the more because, although the will of God, in the principle of loving God and neighbor, is concisely introduced to all believers, since from these two precepts hang the whole law and all the prophets (cf. Mt 22:37-40)—that is, (10) the love of our neighbor which the Lord himself commends to us even to the point of loving our enemies, (11) and we see how many people, already baptized, both confess this truth and venerate it as the Lord's teaching— nevertheless, when they suffer someone's insult, their soul is so seized with desire for revenge and they burn with such torches of hatred that even when the

placari possint; et talibus hominibus iam baptizatis ecclesiae plenae sunt. (12) Quos tamen spirituales viri fraterne admonere non cessant et in spiritu lenitatis instanter instruunt, ut huiusmodi temptationibus occurrere ac resistere parati sint et magis diligant in Christi pace reg-
5 nare quam de inimici oppressione laetari, (13) quod inaniter fieret, si talium peccatorum nulla spes veniae, nulla poenitentiae medicina remaneret. (14) Et certe caveant, qui hoc sentiunt, ne David patriarcham divina electione probatum atque laudatum ignorasse affirment voluntatem dei, cum alienae coniugis amore perculsus etiam maritum
10 eius decipiendum necandumque curavit, de quo tamen scelere, cum esset primo sua, deinde prophetae voce damnatus, poenitendi humilitate et peccati confessione liberatus est. (15) Sed plane vapulavit multa et exemplo suo docuit intelligi non ad sempiternam poenam, sed ad severiorem disciplinam pertinere, quod dictum est a domino: *Qui autem*
15 *novit voluntatem domini sui et facit digna plagis, vapulabit multa.*

19. Nam et illud ad Hebraeos, qui diligentius pertractant, sic intelligunt, ut non de sacrificio contribulati per poenitentiam cordis accipiendum sit, quod dictum est: (2) *Non adhuc pro peccatis relinquitur sacrificium,* sed de sacrificio, de quo tunc loquebatur apostolus, id est
20 holocausto dominicae passionis, quod eo tempore offert quisque pro peccatis suis, quo eiusdem passionis fide dedicatur et christianorum fidelium nomine baptizatus imbuitur, ut hoc significaverit apostolus non posse deinceps eum, qui peccaverit, iterum baptizando purgari. (3) Quo intellectu non intercluditur poenitendi locus, ita sane, ut eos
25 qui baptizati sunt, nondum plenam scientiam veritatis accepisse fateamur. (4) Ex quo conficitur ut omnis, qui scientiam veritatis accepit, etiam baptizatus intelligatur, non autem omnis baptizatus etiam scientiam veritatis acceperit propter quorundam posteriorum provectum vel miserabilem negligentiam, et tamen illud sacrificium de quo
30 loquebatur, id est holocaustum domini, quod tunc pro unoquoque offertur quodammodo cum eius nomine in baptizando signatur, iterum si peccaverit, offerri non potest. (5) Non enim possunt denuo baptizari, qui semel baptizati sunt, quamvis etiam post baptismum per ignorantiam veritatis peccaverint. (6) Ita fit ut, quoniam sine baptismo
35 nemo recte dicitur accepisse scientiam veritatis, omnis qui accepit eam, non ei relinquatur pro peccatis sacrificium, hoc est non possit denuo baptizari; nec tamen omnis, qui non accepit per doctrinam scientiam veritatis debeat arbitrari posse pro se illud offerri sacrificium, si iam oblatum est; id est, (7) si iam eiusdem veritatis per baptismum sacra-
40 menta percepit,

Gospel is brought out and recited to them, they cannot be pacified. The churches are full of such men who are already baptized. (12) Nonetheless, spiritual men do not cease to admonish them fraternally and insistently to instruct in a spirit of gentleness, so that they might be prepared to oppose or resist such temptations and to love to prevail in the peace of Christ more than to rejoice in oppressing an enemy. (13) But all this would be futile were there no hope of pardon for such sinners, no medicine of repentance. (14) And let those who think that no one who sins knowing the will of God has the hope of grace or forgiveness take heed: thinking thus, they affirm that David the patriarch, approved and praised by divine election, had not known the will of God when he, smitten with love for another's wife, took care to deceive and murder her husband, when after he was condemned first by himself and then by the prophet for this wickedness, he obtained pardon through the humiliation of repentance and the confession of sin. (15) But clearly he was severely punished, and by his own example taught that the Lord's saying—"Who knows the will of his lord and does things deserving punishment will be flogged severely"—relates not to eternal punishment, but rather to very harsh discipline (2 Sam. 11–12).

19. Careful perusal of the *Epistle to the Hebrews* leads one to understand that Paul's statement there does not pertain to the sacrifice of the heart bruised by repentance. (2) In saying "there no longer remains a sacrifice for sins" (Heb. 10:26), Paul refers to the sacrificial offering of the Lord's passion that each one offers for his own sins at baptism when, dedicated by faith in that same passion, he is imbued with the name of the Christian faithful. Thus the Apostle indicates here that the person who sins after baptism cannot be cleansed by a second baptism. (3) This understanding leaves open the opportunity for repentance, granted, of course, that we acknowledge that those who are baptized have not yet received the full knowledge of truth. (4) From this one could conclude that everyone who has received the knowledge of truth is considered to be already baptized and, accordingly, that not every baptized person has received the knowledge of truth, whether because of a particular person's having advanced too slowly in catechism or having been unfortunately neglected. Nonetheless, this sacrifice Paul speaks of—that is, the sacrificial offering of the Lord—which is offered in some way for each individual when he is sealed in Christ's name at baptism, cannot again be offered if the man again sins. (5) Thus they who have already been baptized once cannot be baptized again, even though through ignorance of the truth they may have sinned after baptism. (6) And since no one without baptism can rightly be said to have received the knowledge of truth, it then follows that every man who has received such knowledge has no sacrifice for sins left to him, that is, he cannot be baptized a second time. Nor ought anyone who did not receive the knowledge of truth through instruction think that he can receive the divine sacrifice through baptism again if he has already received it once. (7) That is, if he has already taken hold of the sacraments of that same truth by

non potest iterum baptizari, tamquam si diceremus omnem hominem non esse quadrupedem, non ideo tamen omne animal, quod homo non est, etiam quadrupes esse. (8) Eos enim qui iam baptizati fuerint curari melius dicimus per poenitentiam, non renovari, quia renovatio in baptismo est, ubi quidem operatur poenitentia sed tamquam in fundamento. (9) Manente itaque fundamento recurari aedificium potest, si autem fundamentum iterare quis voluerit, totum aedificium subvertat necesse est. (10) Propterea hoc dicit Hebraeis, qui ex novo testamento ad sacerdotium vetus declinasse videbantur: *Ideoque remittentes,* inquit, *initii Christi verbum in consummationem respiciamus non iterum iacientes fundamentum poenitentiae a mortuis operibus et fidei in deum, lavacri doctrinae, impositionis manus, resurrectionis etiam mortuorum et iudicii aeterni.* (11) Ista omnia in baptismo traduntur, quae negat esse repetenda utique in consecrandis fidelibus. Nam in verbi dei tractatione atque doctrina non iterum tantum sed saepius dicenda sunt, sicut rerum, de quibus disseritur, opportunitas flagitat.

20. An vero iam illud occurret, ut non iam, si quodlibet peccatum sciens admiserit, sed si proprie peccatum in spiritum sanctum sciens admiserit, tunc non habere veniam iudicetur. (2) Quo loco quaeri potest, utrum scirent Iudaei per spiritum sanctum operari dominum, quando eum in principe daemoniorum daemonia excludere blasphemabant. (3) Miror autem, quomodo possent in illo spiritum sanctum cognoscere, cum ipsum dominum filium dei esse nescirent in illa scilicet caecitate, *quae ex parte Israel facta est, donec plenitudo gentium intraret.* (4) De qua opportunius suo loco domino adiuvante atque permittente tractabitur. Deinde si diiudicatio spirituum illa intelligitur, qua quisque diiudicat, utrum in quoquam spiritus sanctus an fallaciae spiritus operetur—haec autem diiudicatio certo quodam tempore per spiritum sanctum fidelibus datur, sicut alio loco idem apostolus dicit—(5) quomodo poterant infideles Iudaei sine isto munere diiudicare, utrum per spiritum sanctum dominus operaretur? Et tamen in eis, ut iusta poena ferirentur, apertissima indicia malevolentiae claruerunt, cum et falsos testes in eum compararunt, et submiserunt simulatores qui eum in verbo caperent, (6) et, cum tremenda mirabilia, quae in eius resurrectione facta sunt, eis renuntiarentur, famam falsam disseminare ac veritatem abscondere custodum corruptione conati sunt et alia malitiosi et venenosi animi signa in eis, quantum evangelica narratio demonstrat, apparent.

21. Unde iam velut incepit elucere eum peccare in spiritum sanctum qui operibus, quae per spiritum sanctum fiunt, malivolo animo contradicit. (2) Quamquam enim

baptism, he cannot again be baptized. Just as, for example, if we were to say that no man is four-legged, it would not follow that every animal, since it is not human, would have four legs.[12] (8) And so we say that already-baptized people who sin are better cared for by repentance, not renewal. Renewal comes through baptism, and is the foundation upon which repentance works. (9) With the foundation remaining, a building can be repaired; but if anyone wishes to build the foundation again, the whole edifice must first be torn down. (10) For this reason Paul says to the Hebrews, who apparently had fallen away from the New Testament back into the old priesthood: "Thus leaving aside the elementary doctrines of Christ, let us look to consummation, not again laying the foundation of repentance from dead works, and faith in God, and teaching about cleansing, the laying on of hands, the resurrection of the dead, and eternal judgment" (Heb. 6:1ff.). (11) All such things are handed over at baptism, and it is these things which Paul says ought not be repeated as though for the consecration of the faithful. For in dealing with the word of God and doctrine, such things ought to be said not merely "again," but very often, as circumstances demand.

20. But now someone will think, the point is not whether someone could obtain pardon for knowingly committing just any type of sin, as we have discussed here, but if strictly speaking one can obtain pardon if he knowingly sins against the Holy Spirit. (2) One might ask at this point whether the Jews knew that the Lord worked through the Holy Spirit when they blasphemed, saying he cast out devils in the name of the prince of devils (Mt 9:34). (3) How, I wonder, could they have recognized the Holy Spirit in him? For they did not know he was the Lord and the Son of God because of that blindness "come upon part of Israel until the full number of the Gentiles comes in" (11:25). (4) (We will speak further on this issue in due time, with the Lord's help and permission.) If, then, the ability to distinguish between someone working through the Holy Spirit or through the Spirit of Falsehood is given at some specific time to the faithful by the Holy Spirit, as Paul says elsewhere (1 Cor. 12:10), (5) how then could the unfaithful Jews, without this gift, have judged whether the Lord worked through the Holy Spirit? But, nonetheless, they were struck with a just penalty, for they gave the most obvious proofs of their malevolence, arranging false witness against the Lord and producing hypocrites who trapped him with words (Mt 22:15–17), (6) and, when the great wonders done at his resurrection were reported to them, they attempted to spread false rumors and to hide the truth by bribing the guards (Mt 28:11–13). Indeed, the Gospel story gives many other examples of their malice and slander.

---

12. That is, though no one who is not baptized can properly be said to have the knowledge of truth, it does not follow that a baptized person who has not learned the truth can be considered unbaptized.

nesciat, utrum ille sit spiritus sanctus, tamen, qui hoc animo est, ut ea opera, quibus invidet, malit non esse spiritus sancti, non quia mala sunt sed quia invidet eis, quia ipsi bonitati est contrarius per malitiam suam, recte in spiritum sanctum peccare iudicatur. (3) Verumtamen si*
5 ex eo quoque hominum numero, quibus dominus illud crimen obicit, veniens ad fidem Christi et poenitendi cruciatibus edomita invidia salutem cum lacrimis poscens sicut etiam nonulli eorum fortasse fecerunt, quaero utrum quisquam tanto errore crudescat, ut aut neget eos ad Christi baptismum admitti oportuisse aut frustra admissos esse conten-
10 dat. (4) Nam si quisquis per invidiam opera divina blasphemat, quoniam bonis dei, hoc est donis dei malitia sua resistit, in spiritum sanctum peccare et propterea spem veniae non habere existimandus est. Attendamus utrum ex eo numero fuerit idem apostolus Paulus. (5) Dicit enim: *Qui prius fui blasphemus et persecutor et iniuriosus, sed*
15 *misericordiam consecutus sum, quia ignorans feci in incredulitate.* (6) An forte ideo non pertinuit ad hoc genus criminis, quia non erat invidus. (7) Audiamus quid alibi dicat: *Fuimus enim,* inquit, *et nos stulti aliquando et increduli, errantes, servientes voluptatibus et desideriis variis, in malitia et invidia agentes, abhominabiles, invicem odio habentes.*
20 **22.** Si ergo nec paganis nec Hebraeis nec haereticis aut scismaticis nondum baptizatis ad baptismum Christi aditus clauditur, ubi condemnata vita priore in melius commutentur, quamvis christianitati et ecclesiae dei adversantes, antequam christianis sacramentis abluerentur, etiam spiritui sancto, quanta potuerunt infestatione, restiterint; (2) si
25 etiam hominibus, qui usque ad sacramentorum perceptionem veritatis scientiam perceperunt et post haec lapsi spiritui sancto restiterunt, ad sanitatem redeuntibus et pacem dei poenitendo quaerentibus auxilium misericordiae non negatur; (3) si denique de illis ipsis, quibus blasphemiam in spiritum sanctum ab eis prolatam dominus obiecit, si
30 qui resipiscentes ad dei gratiam confugerunt, sine ulla dubitatione sanati sunt, quid aliud restat nisi ut peccatum in spiritum sanctum, quod neque in hoc saeculo neque in futuro dimitti dominus dicit, nullum intelligatur nisi perseverantia in nequitia et in malignitate cum desperatione indulgentiae dei. (4) Hoc est enim gratiae illius et paci
35 resistere, de quibus nobis sermo nunc ortus est. Nam hinc licet advertere etiam ipsis Iudaeis, quorum blasphemiam dominus arguit, non fuisse clausum corrigendi se et poenitendi locum, quod idem dominus in ea ipsa reprehensione ait illis: *Aut facite arborem bonam et fructum eius bonum, aut facite arborem malam et fructum eius malum.* (5) Quod
40 utique nulla ratione diceretur eis, si propter illam blasphemiam iam commutare animum in melius et recte factorum fructus generare non possent aut frustra etiam sine

---

* The subordinate clause beginning with *si* has no main verb; *aut neget eos* suggests a plural subject: cf. *si qui resipiscentes* in 22,3.

21. It now begins to be clear, then, that he sins against the Holy Spirit who speaks maliciously against the works done by the Spirit. (2) For even though one might not know whether a certain wonder is worked by the Holy Spirit, nevertheless, if he has such a character that he simply chooses not to believe that the Spirit did these works—not because they are evil, but because he in his malice opposes goodness itself—he is rightly considered as sinning against the Holy Spirit. (3) Nonetheless, if from that number of men whom the Lord charged with this sin some came to the faith of Christ, having conquered this hatred by the torments of repentance and with tears begging for salvation (as some of them perhaps did do), would anyone err so greatly and be so harsh as to deny that such persons should have been admitted to the baptism of Christ, or to contend that they were baptized in vain? (4) For if anyone through hatred blasphemes divine works because his own malice resists the goods (that is, the gifts) of God, he should be considered to have sinned against the Holy Spirit, and therefore not to have hope of pardon. Let us consider whether the apostle Paul himself once numbered among such men. (5) For he says: "I, who once blasphemed and persecuted and insulted, attained mercy, because I acted ignorantly in unbelief" (1 Tim. 1:13). (6) Perhaps this is not relevant to this type of crime, since Paul was not hateful. (7) But let us hear what he says elsewhere: "For we ourselves were once foolish and unbelieving, erring, slave to various pleasures and desires, leading our lives in malice and envy, hated by other men and in turn hating them" (Tit. 3:3).

22. Is access to baptism in Christ then ever denied to pagans or Jews or heretics or unbaptized schismatics, no matter how hostile they had been towards Christianity and towards the Church of God before they were cleansed by the Christian sacraments, no matter how noisily they had resisted even the Holy Spirit when, condemning their former life, they change for the better? (2) To even those men who, having perceived the knowledge of truth and even receiving the sacraments, later lapsed and resisted the Holy Spirit, once they return to sanity and seek the peace of God by repentance, is the aid of mercy ever denied? (3) Were not those very men whom the Lord charged with blasphemy against the Holy Spirit, once some came to their senses and sought refuge in the grace of God, without any hesitation healed? What remains then except to say that the sin against the Holy Spirit, which the Lord says is forgiven neither in this world nor in the one to come, is to be understood as nothing other than continuing in wickedness and maliciousness with despair of the kindness and mercy of God. (4) For this is to resist the peace and grace of God, the topic that occasioned our discussion. And we should attend here to the fact that the Lord himself left open the opportunity for correction and repentance to those same Jews whose blasphemy he condemned. He indicated as much when he reproached them, saying: "Either make the tree good and its fruits good, or make the tree bad and its fruits bad" (Mt 12:33). (5) Why would he conceivably have said this to them if their blasphemy had made

peccati sui dimissione generarent.

23. Ergo quia dominus in spiritu dei expellebat daemonia ceterosque humanorum corporum morbos languoresque sanabat non ob aliud nisi ut crederetur dicenti sibi: *Agite poenitentiam. Appropinquabit enim reg-*
5 *num caelorum*—(2) invisibiliter enim peccata dimittuntur, cui dimissioni fidem miraculis comparabat, quod in illo paralytico manifestissime ostenditur. (3) Cum enim primo ei donum invisible obtulisset, propter quod venerat (non enim iam venerat filius hominis ut iudicaret saeculum sed ut salvaret mundum) cum ergo dixisset: (4) *Dimissa sunt tibi*
10 *peccata,* murmuratumque esset a Iudaeis indignantibus, quod eis tantam potestatem sibi arrogasse videretur: *Quid est,* inquit, *facilius dicere: Dimissa sunt tibi peccata, an dicere: Surge et ambula? Ut sciatis autem, quia potestatem habet filius hominis dimittere peccata (ait paralytico): Tibi dico, surge, tolle grabatum tuum et vade in domum tuam.* (5) Quo facto et
15 quibus dictis satis declaravit ideo se illa facere in corporibus, ut crederetur animas peccatorum dimissione liberare, id est ut de potestate visibili potestas invisibilis mereretur fidem—(6) quia ergo in spiritu dei faciebat illa omnia, ut gratiam pacemque hominibus largiretur, gratiam in dimissione peccatorum, pacem in reconciliatione dei, a quo separant
20 sola peccata, cum dixissent Iudaei quod in Beelzebub eiceret daemonia, misericorditer eos voluit admonere, ne verbum dicerent et blasphemiam in spiritum sanctum, hoc est ne gratiae dei pacique resisterent, quam per spiritum sanctum donare dominus venerat, (7) non quia iam hoc fecerant, quod sibi neque in hoc saeculo neque in
25 futuro dimitteretur, sed ne desperando de venia aut quasi de sua iustitia praesumendo et poenitentiam non agendo aut perseverando in peccatis hoc facerent. Hoc modo enim dicerent verbum, hoc est blasphemiam in spiritum sanctum in quo dominus signa illa propter largiendam gratiam pacemque faciebat, si perseverantia peccatorum ipsi
30 gratiae pacique resisterent. (8) Verbum enim dicere non ita videtur hic positum, ut tantummodo illud intelligatur, quod per linguam fabricamus, sed quod corde conceptum etiam opere exprimimus. (9) Sicut enim non confitentur deum qui tantum oris sono confitentur, non etiam bonis operibus—nam de his dictum est: *Confitentur enim se nosse*
35 *deum, factis autem negant;* ex quo manifestum est dici aliquid factis, sicut manifestum est negari aliquid factis—(10) et sicut illud quod ait apostolus: *Nemo dicit dominus Iesus nisi in spiritu sancto,* non potest recte intelligi nisi ut factis dicere intelligatur—(11) non enim hoc in spiritu sancto dicere putandi sunt, quibus ipse dominus dicit: *Utquid mihi*

them unable to change for the better and to produce the fruits of good deeds, or if they could only produce them in vain without forgiveness for their own sins?

23. Therefore the Lord expelled demons and cured other sicknesses and weaknesses of the human body by the Spirit of God for no other reason than to inspire belief as he cried out: "Repent, for the Kingdom of Heaven has drawn near" (Mt 3:2)—(2) for sins are forgiven invisibly, and he was inspiring faith in this forgiveness by performing these miracles, as the case of the paralytic most clearly shows. (3) For when to fulfill his purpose in coming (for the Son of Man had not yet come to judge the world, but to save it), he had first given this invisible gift to the paralytic, saying: (4) "Your sins are forgiven you," the Jews murmured against him, angry because they thought he seemed to claim such great power for himself. "What," he then asked, "is easier to say? 'Your sins are forgiven you' or 'Arise and walk'? But so that you might know that the Son of Man has the power to forgive sins (he said to the paralytic) I say to you, arise, take up your cot and go into your house" (Mk 2:9–11). (5) By this deed and word he declared that he worked these bodily miracles so that people would believe that he also freed the souls of sinners by forgiveness, that is, so that from the visible power of healing the invisible power of forgiveness would merit faith. (6) Since therefore he did all these things by the Spirit of God, so that he might bestow grace and peace on men, grace in the forgiveness of sinners, peace in their reconciliation to God from whom sins alone separated them, when the Jews had said he drove out demons in the name of Beelzebub, he wanted to admonish them out of mercy, lest they speak a word and so blaspheme against the Holy Spirit, that is, lest they resist the grace and peace of God which the Lord had come to give to men through the Holy Spirit. (7) He spoke to them, then, not because they had already blasphemed against the Holy Spirit and so would never be forgiven, but rather to warn them lest, despairing of pardon, or assuming that God's justice was like theirs and so not repenting, or continuing in their sins, they do such a thing. For by so acting they would speak a word (that is, blaspheme) against the Holy Spirit, by whom the Lord performed those signs in order to bestow grace and peace, if by persevering in their sins they resisted grace and peace. (8) For in this context, "to say a word" need not be taken to indicate only what we fashion with our tongue, but rather what, conceived in our heart, we bring to expression in deed. (9) So also, they do not acknowledge God who confess only with the sound of their mouths but not with good works. Concerning this sort of person, Paul said: "They confess that they know God, but they deny it by their deeds" (Tit. 1:16), from which it is clear that, just as deeds can deny something, so too they can express something. (10) And likewise the Apostle's statement, "No one says 'Jesus is Lord' except by the Holy Spirit" (1 Cor. 12:3), cannot be rightly understood unless "to say" is understood in the sense of "saying with deeds." (11) For such people, whose mouths say one thing but whose deeds

dicitis: domine, domine, et non facitis quae dico vobis, et illud: *Non omnis qui dicit mihi: domine, domine, intrabit in regnum caelorum*——(12) sic etiam, qui hoc verbum, quod sine venia vult intelligi dominus, in spiritum sanctum dicit, hoc est, qui desperans de gratia et pace, quam donat, in peccatis suis perseverandum sibi esse dicit, dicere intelligendus est factis ut, quomodo illi factis deum negant, sic isti factis dicant se in mala vita sua et perditis moribus perseveraturos, ut etiam ita faciant, hoc est perseverent. (13) Quod si faciunt, quis iam miretur aut quis non intelligat et dominum Iesum Christum per illam comminationem ad poenitentiam vocasse Iudaeos, ut eis in se credentibus gratiam pacemque donaret, et huic gratiae pacique resistentibus et hoc modo verbum atque blasphemiam in spiritum sanctum dicentibus, hoc est in peccatis suis desperata atque impia mentis obstinatione perseverantibus et adversus deum sine humilitate confessionis atque poenitentiae superbientibus neque in hoc saeculo neque in futuro veniam posse concedi? (14) Quae si ita sunt opportunitate tractandi de gratia et pace, quae nobis est a deo patre et domino nostro Iesu Christo, magna et difficillima eodem ipso domino largiente quaestio dissoluta est. (15) Quisquis autem adhuc de re tanta diligentiorem considerationem tractationemque desiderat, in evangelii tractatione atque in verbis evangelistarum sibi desideranda esse cognoscat et meminerit nos nunc epistolam Pauli apostoli ad Romanos suscepisse tractandam, cuius epistolae textum consequentem in aliis voluminibus, si dominus voluerit, vestigabimus, ut huius iam tandem iste sit modus.

say the opposite, should not be thought to mouth this confession by the Holy Spirit. The Lord himself says to these people: "Why do you call me 'Lord, Lord' and not do what I tell you?" (Lk 6:46) and "Not everyone who says to me 'Lord, Lord' will enter the kingdom of heaven" (Mt 7:21). (12) Thus they speak against the Holy Spirit (which the Lord wants us to understand is without pardon) who, despairing of the grace and peace which Christ gives, claim that they must continue in their sins. They claim this by their deeds so that as in the first case, when the Jews denied God by their deeds, so here in the same way these men say by their deeds that they will continue in their evil life and depraved ways, and so they do; that is, they continue. (13) And so if they conduct themselves like this, who now wonders or fails to understand that the Lord Jesus Christ had called the Jews to repentance precisely by this threat, so that he might give grace and peace to those believing in him? and that these people resisting this grace and peace and thus blaspheming against the Holy Spirit, that is, continuing in their sins with despairing and impious stubborness of mind and proudly opposing God without the humility of confession and penitence—that these people cannot be pardoned either in this world or in the one to come? (14) If this is so, then by this occasion of treating the issue of grace and peace, which we have from God the Father and our Lord Jesus Christ, a great and most difficult question, with the help of our Lord, has been resolved. (15) Moreover, if anyone now desires a more diligent consideration and treatment of this very important issue, he should understand that what he wants will be found in the treatment of the Gospel and in the words of the evangelists; and he should recall that we have undertaken here to treat the letter of Paul the Apostle to the Romans. And we will trace out the rest of this letter's literal content in other volumes, if the Lord wills it, so that, finally, we might come to the end of this one.

Appendix

ADDENDA AND CORRIGENDA TO *CSEL 84*

The following list gives the differences noted between the lessons of the manuscripts I consulted and the readings as reported in Divjak's critical apparatus. The numbers refer to the page and line in the *CSEL* edition.

Expositio quarundam propositionum ex epistola ad Romanos:
manuscript *A* = *Codex Parisinus Latinus 1449 nouv. acqu.*, 64r.-72v.

- 4: 18. sibi, *om.*
  - 20. convenirent] oportet
  - 22. illorum] eorum
  - 23. de] a; sui] eorum
- 5: 7. impedientes personas] impedientis personae
  - 12. qui, *om.*
- 6: 8. nos reprehenderit] nos non reprehendat
  - 12. utique, *om.*
  - 15. quod] quo
  - 17. ait
- 7: 6. *post* esse *add.* cum
  - 8. volumus] nolumus
  - 9. affligimur] adfligimur; hic] hoc
  - 14. quisque] quisquam; se, *om.*
  - 16. et, *om.*; vehementiore] vehementiori
  - 20. liberatoris auxilium] auxilium liberatoris
- 8: 6. oboediendo] oboediendum
  - 7. ista] ita; de, *om.* [Hence *A* reads "ita desideria carnis," i.e., it establishes the reading of *d*].
  - 16. Iesum Christum] spiritum Iesum
- 9: 8. iustitiam] iustitia
  - 9. per legem, *om.*
  - 14. *post* cum *add.* autem
  - 24. et poenam
- 12: 25. qua] quo
- 13: 5. abundaret] habundaret
  - 11. abundavit] habundavit
  - 20. superabundasse] superhabundasse
- 15: 3. mortali, *om.*
  - 11-12. ab ea re, *om.*
  - 18. liberationem] liberandum
  - 19. vehementiore] vehementiori

16:	14.	enim, *om.*
	19.	fiat] faciat
	22.	consequentibus] sequentibus
17:	9.	est, *om.*
	11.	sit, *om.*
	12.	imagine] imaginem
	16.	*post* maiores *add.* enim
	23.	dixit] dicit
18:	5.	supra] super
	10.	a] ab; facit
	11.	legi] legem
	13.	iam non] nec
	17.	accepta] accepto
	17–18.	dulcedine] dulcedinis
	21.	enim] autem
19:	8.	psalmis] psalmo
	11.	odi] odio
	15–16.	homo describitur] homo dei scribitur
	16.	peccatis] peccator
20:	5.	damnatio] dominatio
	7.	desint talia] sint alia
	8.	iam, *om.*
	10.	ut] et
	21.	Adae conditionem] ad conditionem
21:	2.	in, *om.*
	16.	essent implenda quoniam, *om.*
	24.	noster dominus] dominus noster
	25.	venit in, *om.*
22:	2.	vocat] vocans
23:	1–4.	qua...prudentia, *om.*
	5.	*post* dei *add.* non
	6.	prudentia] prudentiam
	10.	elegit] elegit diligit
	13–14.	quomodo...potest, *om.*
	22–24.	Si spiritus...vobis, *om.*
	25.	vivificabit] vivificavit
24:	14.	quis] quid
	22.	non, *om.*
	24.	nondum] nam cum
25:	1.	adoptionem] adoptionis
	2.	qui ei, *om.*
	3.	traditus fuerit] traditur
	8.	nondum] nec dum

	13.	et spiritus, *om.*
	14.	commutatus] commutamus
	19.	a timore mortis vindicat] timorem mortis vincat
	20.	qui] in; terrore] errore
26:	12.	animalis quae, *om.*
	15.	spiritu, *om.*
	24–25.	in homine] supra
27:	1.	psalmo] psalmis
	2.	de vanitate] de qua vanitate
	4.	abundantia] habuntantia; quo] quem
	11.	eam, *om.*
	13–20.	etiam...ut et, *om.*
	20.	ipsa perveniat] ipsi perveniant
	22.	refert] referes
	24.	subiacebant] subiacent
28:	5.	sollicitationes] sollicitudines
	8–14.	non solum...ingemiscimus, *om.*
29:	12.	quando] quae
	13.	vel emendationem, *om.*
	15.	intelligitur] intellegetur
	16.	nos, *om.*
	18.	etiam] et
	19–20.	et nomen...inveni, *om.*
30:	1.	faciat] facit
	8.	autem, *om.*
	9–15.	manifestum...sunt, *om.*
	16.	vocati...propositum, *om.*
	18–19.	et secuturum] cunctorum
	19.	suam, *om.*
	22.	dicit] ait
	25.	et naturaliter est filius] naturaliter et filius
31:	16.	sint] sunt
	20.	appetunter] adpetuntur
	22.	et, *om.*
	23.	enim, *om.*
32:	1.	qui, *om.*
	2.	qui, *om.*
	5.	de caelo, *om.*
	8.	eos] eas
	12.	intelligi] intellegi
	19.	id est, *om.*
	20.	nos, *om.*

33:	2.	rationales] rationabiles
	8.	*post* aeternitatem *add.* et
	15.	intelligerent] intellegerent
	27.	*post* ante *add.* quam
34:	14–17.	Quid ergo...electio, *om.*
	17–19.	enim omnes...non quidem, *om.*; *add. in marg.*
	19–20.	deus elegit opera] eligit deus opera
	22.	*ante* quia *add.* qua propter; in eum, *om.*
35:	1–2.	quae ipsa...praescientia, *om.*
	10.	qui] quia
	22–23.	misericors fuero] misericordiam praestabo
36:	1.	nos, *om.*
	10.	illos] illum
	10–12.	nostrum enim...bene operandi, *om.*
	15.	miserentes] miserantes
	16.	voluntatis, *om.*
37:	2.	dei esse] esse dei
	6.	ut, *om.*
	17–18.	elegit...quos, *om.*
	20.	etiam] et
	21.	Et] ut
	24.	cuius] cui
38:	5.	cum tamen homini, *om.*
	11.	ut, *om.*
	12.	viris, *om.*
	17–18.	et istorum...operentur, *om.*
	22.	O homo, *om.*
39:	2.	honorem] honore; contumeliam] contumelia
	5.	iudiceris] iudicaris
	10.	inquit, *om.*
	11.	feci vobis] vobis feci
	14.	conteres eos] conterendum est
	15.	*post* homine *om.* et
	17.	et, *om.*
	19.	honorem] honore
	20.	quisquis] si
	21.	et, *om.*
40:	3.	Pharaone] Pharaonem
	4.	meritis] merito; superioris impietatis] superiori impietati
	11.	in, *om.*
	15.	operamur] opera
	18.	si, *om.*
41:	17.	est, *om.*
	20.	et in corde tuo, *om.*
	24.	ore

42:	1.	in] ad
	3.	faciet] fecit
	17.	iustitiae] iustitias
	18.	ut] unde
43:	1.	qui sunt ex Israel, hi sunt] qui ex Israel hii sunt
	12.	prodesset] prodest
	16.	debent] debeant
44:	8.	per] post
	24.	subditos esse potestatibus] esse potestatibus subditos
45:	7.	aut, *om.*
	8–12.	versatur...errorem, *om.*
	12.	dominus] deus
	17.	potestatis] potestates
	21.	*post* vis *om.* autem
	24.	numquid, *om.*
46:	3.	laudabit...et, *om.*
	4–5.	sive...illa, *om.*
	5.	laudem habebis] habebis laudem
	17.	non, *om.*
47:	16.	spectat] expectat
	19.	Et, *om.*
	21.	culpandam] culpam
48:	7.	firmitate] infirmitate
	9.	Ideo sequitur] id consequitur
	11.	olus] holus
	12.	secundum] se secundum
49:	4.	in, *om.*
	22.	iterim] iam
50:	4.	non solum] novit
	5.	sed...ergo, *om.*
	6.	abundet] habundet
	18.	penes] paenes
51:	2–3.	veritatem dei] caritatem Christi
	4.	autem, *om.*
	5.	intelligat] intellegat deum; gentes dominum] dominum gentes
	11–12.	etiam ipsa] ipsa etiam
	15.	intelligunt] intellegunt; sua, *om.*
	16.	si, *om.*
	22.	*post* intelligitur *add.* ut
52:	9.	*post* neque *add.* aliter

Epistolae ad Romanos inchoata expositio:
manuscript *O = Codex Oxoniensis Laud misc. 134,* 1r–14v.

146:	2.	uti] ut
	7.	connectit] conectit
147:	6.	se, *om.*
	7.	prophetarum] profetarum
	13.	inquit] in quid
	17.	crederem] crederetur
148:	5.	a] ab
	11.	quisquam
	15.	omnis] omnes
	17.	asserat] adferat
	24.	quod, *om.*
149:	8.	cui] cum
	11.	quia] qui
	13.	prophetas] phetas
	22.	mutatum et] est
150:	25.	consurrexistis] conresurrexistis
151:	8–10.	dei...filium David, *add. in marg.*
152:	4.	David] Davit
153:	17.	inquit, *om.*
	23.	meritis] merito
154:	7.	inquit] inquid
	12–13.	Iesu Christi] Christi Iesu
155:	2.	et, *om.*
	20.	qua reconciliamur] quare conciliamur
157:	6.	*post* etiam *add.* iustitia
	8.	sacris scripturis] scripturis sacris
	21.	impius] iniquus
158:	3.	et, *om.*
	6.	in, *om.*
	20.	a] ab
159:	6.	a, *om.*
	7.	nostro, *om.*
	20.	quoquo modo] quomodo
160:	5.	seiungebamur] separemur
161:	17.	arbitror] arbitrar
	20.	*post* punice *add.* loquis
162:	10.	Chananaea] Cananea
	16.	Chananaeam] Cananeam
163:	10.	*post* dominus *add.* non
	11–12.	filium...adversus, *om.*
	24.	impietatis] pietatis; aspergat] adspargat

Appendix

164: 5–6.   spiritum sanctum] sanctum spiritum
      23.   sanctum, *om.*
165: 7.   spiritum sanctum] sanctum spiritum
166: 4.   lapidantium] lapidabant
      19.   putans] putens
      25.   umquam] umquem
167: 1.   corrigat] corrigeret; ampuavit] conputabit
      2.   quae] qui
      11.   verbis] versis
      15.   ipse, *om.*
      25.   prophetas] profetas
168: 8.   adversus] adversum
      15–16.   quia...ignosci, *add. in marg.*
      19.   si, *om.*
169: 8.   quid] quod
      10.   negligenter] neglegenter
      15.   deputare] depurari
      24.   peccare, *om.*
170: 2.   coniuge] coiuge
      12.   *post* si *add.* a
      18.   quod enim] hoc enim
171: 4–5.   tamquam...vapulabit, *add. in marg.*
172: 2.   accedit] accidit
      13.   spirituales] spiritales
173: 2.   vapulavit] vapulabit
      17.   nondum] non
174: 7.   id est] ita est
      10–11.   quadrupes] quadripede
175: 1.   non iam si] non si
      16.   diiudicare] rediiudicare
176: 4.   incepit] incipit
177: 12.   *post* perceptionem *add.* et
      13.   perceperunt] pervenerunt
178: 3.   et] ac
      13.   regnum caelorum] regnum dei
      15.   manifestissime] apertissime
      23.   ait] dicit
179: 14.   aut] ac
180: 6–8.   non...dicere, *add. in marg.*
      18.   Quod si faciunt, *deleti*
181: 7.   deo patre et domino nostro Iesu Christo] deo patre nostro et domino Iesu Christo

Index of names

In the references following each entry, the bold-face number refers to the paragraph number of the commentary; the numbers which follow, to the sentences within that paragraph. Where the first sentence of a paragraph is referred to, a "1" will appear in the index entry, though in the text of the commentary itself the first sentence is not numbered.

PROPOSITIONS

Abraham: **20**:1; **25**:1; **65**:2; **69**:1,2
Adam: **29**:1,2,3,4,6,10; **45–46**:7
Athenians: **3**:3
Caesar: **72**:5
Christ: **1**:1; **2**:1; **13–18**:11;
  27–28:3; **29**:4,7; **32–34**:4,5; **36**:3;
  45–46:5; **47**:1; **48**:4,5; **51**:1; **53**:6;
  57:1; **58**:2,4,6; **59**:1,2,4; **60**:13;
  65:2; **68**:3; **82**:1; **83**:1; **84**:4
Christian: **72**:4
David: **53**:11; **59**:2,3,4
Hosea: **64**:1; **65**:2
Isaiah: **65**:1,2
Israel: **65**:1,2; **69**:2; **82**:3
Jacob: **60**:1; **61**:1
Moses: **29**:3; **32–34**:1,5; **68**:1
Paul: **1**:1; **5**:1; **7–8**:1; **9**:1; **12**:1;
  13–18:5; **21**:1; **26**:1; **29**:5,7,9;
  30:1; **31**:1; **32–34**:3,4; **35**:2;
  36:1,3,5; **37**:4; **40**:1,4; **42**:2; **43**:1;
  45–46:4,7; **48**:2,6; **49**:1,2,6; **51**:1;
  52:1; **53**:11,13,15,16; **54**:1;
  55:2,3,4; **56**:1,4; **57**:3; **58**:1,8;
  60:2; **61**:1; **62**:1,14,17,18,19;
  63:1; **64**:1; **66**:1; **67**:2; **68**:2,3;
  69:1; **70**:1; **72**:1; **73**:4; **74**:2; **75**:1;
  76:1; **78**:2; **79**:1,2; **80**:1,4; **81**:1;
  82:1; **83**:1; **84**:1,4
Pharaoh: **62**:5,6,7,8; **63**:1

INCHOATA

Athenians: **3**:4
Christ: **1**:1,2,3,4; **2**:1; **3**:1,3,5;
  4:2,3,4,5,7,8,10,12;
  5:2,3,5,9,10,11,13,14,15,17;
  6:2,3,4; **7**:1,2,4; **8**:1,4,6; **10**:5;
  11:1,5; **12**:2,3,4,5,7,8,9; **14**:6,8;
  15:4,16; **17**:1; **18**:5,12; **19**:4,10;
  21:3; **22**:1; **23**:12,13,14
Christian: **10**:5; **16**:7; **17**:4; **19**:2;
  22:1
Christianity: **22**:1
Cornelius: **18**:7
Cumaean: **3**:3,4
David: **4**:2,3,4,5,6,7,8,9;
  5:1,5,6,7,8,9,10; **7**:2; **10**:9; **18**:14
Hebrew(s): **4**:2; **11**:3; **18**:2; **19**:1,10
Israel: **20**:3
Job: **10**:4
Nathan: **10**:9
Paul: **1**:1,3,4; **2**:4; **3**:2; **4**:2,4,7,8,12;
  5:1,11,12,15; **6**:1,2,3,4; **7**:1,3,5,7;
  8:1; **10**:4,7; **11**:3,4; **12**:5; **14**:1;
  15:6; **18**:2; **19**:1,2,4,10,11; **20**:4;
  21:4,6; **23**:9,15
Peter: **10**:5,6,8,10; **12**:2; **15**:10;
  16:6; **18**:7
Punic: **13**:1,3,5,6
Roman(s): **1**:1; **3**:3; **13**:6; **23**:15
Samaritan(s): **15**:7,8
Sibyl: **3**:3
Simon: **15**:10; **16**:6
Stephen: **15**:5,6
Valerius: **13**:1,2
Vergil: **3**:3

Index of words

PROPOSITIONS

adoption: 52:1,2,4,7,8; 53:1,19,20; 56:3
angel: 58:3
apostle: 10:1; 60:2
authority: 52:5; 72:1,2,4,6; 73:1,2,3; 74:1,2
blaspheme: 52:5
bodily: 77:1
body: 13-18:10,11; 32-34:1,4; 35:1; 36:5; 45-46:5; 50:1; 51:1,2,3; 52:5; 53:1,4,20,21; 72:2
call: 55:4; 60:1,14,15; 64:1; 66:1
carnal: 41:1; 45-46:1,3,6; 47:1
circumcision: 11:1; 24:1; 82:1
command: 29:2; 38:1,2; 40:4; 74:2
commandment: 37:1; 39:1,3; 52:3,4
concupiscence: 13-18fR:2; 30:3; 37:1,2,3; 45-46:7; 47:2
condemn: 10:1; 13-18:3; 81:2
condemnation: 29:4,5,10; 45-46:3; 47:1; 53:12
confess: 59:1; 67:1
confession: 59:2; 67:3; 80:2
conscience: 10:1; 74:2; 75:4; 78:2,4
consent: 7-8:1; 35:1,2; 36:4
correction: 80:5
create: 49:1; 84:1
creation: 3:2; 53:,5,8,11,13,14,17,18
creature: 53:3,13; 58:8,9
custom: 45-46:1,3
damnation: 60:14
dead: 1:1; 13-18:11; 36:3; 37:4; 38:2; 40:2,3; 50:6; 51:2; 56:4,5; 67:2
death: 29:2,3,4,7,9; 35:5; 36:2; 37:4; 40:3,2; 43:2; 45-46:5; 48:4,5,6; 50:1; 52:2,6,9; 53:3,13,14; 58:1,2
deed: 73:3
desire: 13-18:6,9; 36:2; 39:1; 54:7; 66:1
despair: 80:5
devil: 42:1
election: 60:1,4,8
evil: 7-8:1; 13-18:3; 49:3; 60:1,2,3; 62:9,12,13,16; 71:2; 73:4; 84:3
faith: 3:5; 19:1,2; 20:2; 21:2; 24:1; 30:2; 53:13,14,18,20; 58:1; 59:1; 60:9,11; 62:9,12,15,16; 67:1,3; 68:2,3; 72:5; 75:4; 78:1; 81:2; 82:4; 84:2
fault: 48:3; 62:14
foreknew: 55:3; 60:4,11
foreknowledge: 55:4; 60:4,11; 62:15
freedom: 60:2; 62:1
Gentile: 7-8:2
gift: 11:1; 21:1; 26:1; 29:4,5; 60:5,6,10; 62:1,9,13
glorify: 82:1
glory: 13-18:13; 20:1; 25:1; 26:1; 53:6; 57:2; 60:6; 64:1
God: 2:1; 3:1; 4:1,2; 5:1; 6:2; 9:1,2; 10:1; 12:1; 13-18:8,11,13; 20:1,2; 21:2; 24:1; 25:1; 26:1; 35:1; 36:4; 41:1; 44:2,3; 45-46:5,6; 47:2; 48:2; 49:1,2,4,6; 50:2; 52:4; 53:1,5,6,7,8,13,14,16,18,20; 54:2,3,4,6,7; 55:3,4; 56:2; 58:1,2,7,8,9; 59:1,3; 60:1,2,3,4,6,7,9,10,11,12,15; 61:1,2,3,4,5,6,7; 62:1,3,4,6,7,9,10,13,15,18,19,20,22,23; 63:1,2; 64:2; 66:3; 67:2,3; 69:1,2; 72:1,3,5,6; 73:3,4; 75:2; 76:1; 79:1,2,3; 80:1; 81:2; 82:1; 83:1,2; 84:2
Gospel: 2:1; 60:13; 64:1; 65:3; 76:1; 82:2; 83:1
grace: 2:1; 3:5;

13-18:2,3,5,6,7,8,12; 20:2; 21:2;
26:1; 27-28:1; 29:4,5,6,7,8; 30:2;
31:1,2; 35:1,2; 36:2; 37:2,3,5;
41:1; 44:2,3; 45-46:2,4,5,6; 47:2;
48:2,9; 52:2,4,6; 60:13,14
guilt: 52:6
heart: 62:6,7,8; 63:1; 66:1; 67:1;
75:1; 78:1; 79:1
hope: 49:4; 51:2; 53:12,13; 58:5;
66:1
idolatry: 3:2; 68:2,3
idols: 78:2,3; 82:4
immortality: 51:2
impiety: 3:1,5; 60:2;
62:9,12,13,15,16; 63:1,2
impious: 22:1
Jesus: 13-18:11; 29:4,7; 32-34:5;
45-46:5; 47:1; 48:4; 51:1; 67:1;
83:1
Jewish: 2:1; 67:3; 70:3
Jews: 30:1; 59:2; 60:13; 64:1,2;
66:1,2; 68:2; 69:3; 70:1,3; 82:1,2;
84:3
Judaism: 82:4
justice: 13-18:7
justification: 29:5,10; 55:2
kingdom: 72:3,6
law: 7-8:2; 9:2; 11:1;
13-18:1,2,3,5,6,7; 19:1,2; 20:1;
23:1; 25:1; 27-28:1,2,3; 29:2,3;
30:1,2,3; 35:1,2; 36:1,2,3,4;
37:3,4,5; 38:1; 40:2,4; 41:1,2;
44:1,2,3; 45-46:2,4,6,7; 47:2;
48:1,2,3,6,7,8,9; 49:1,2,4,6; 50:2;
52:2,3,4,6; 53:16; 68:3;
75:1,2,3,4
Liberator: 13-18:7,12; 37:2; 44:3;
45-46:4; 48:4; 52:4,9
life: 13-18:8,11; 29:3,4,7,8,10;
30:2; 36:5; 50:1; 51:1,2; 53:4,6;
54:2,4,6,7; 58:1,2,3; 60:11,15;
72:1,2,3; 74:1
Lord: 3:1; 4:2; 9:2; 29:3,4,6;
32-34:2,3,5; 42:2; 45-46:5;
48:4,5,6,7; 54:5,7; 56:1;
59:1,2,3,4; 62:20; 65:1,3; 67:1,2;
69:3; 71:1; 72:1,5; 74:2; 75:2;
78:2; 80:3,4; 82:1,3; 84:4
love: 2:1; 13-18:8; 26:1; 44:3;
45-46:4; 48:3,8,9; 52:1; 53:11;
54:4,7; 57:1; 58:1,7,8;
60:5,6,7,9,10; 61:4,5,7; 62:22;
71:1,2; 74:2; 75:1,2,3,4
lust: 13-18:3
mercy: 61:1,2,3; 62:1,2,4,11,12,13;
64:1,2; 67:3; 82:1; 83:2
merit: 20:2; 60:8,14,15; 62:9,12;
64:1
mortality: 13-18:10; 29:1; 50:2
nature: 37:3; 45-46:7; 49:1,5; 56:2;
60:14
obedience: 29:10; 72:6
obey: 13-18:9; obey: 35:1; 36:4;
45-46:4,6; 62:8
offense: 30:3; 37:3; 40:3,4;
pardon: 31:1
peace: 13-18:2,10,11,12,13; 51:3;
53:21
pleasure: 42:1
predestination: 55:4
predestine: 55:4
pride: 4:1; pride: 66:2; 72:1
promise: 58:3
providence: 52:3,4
redemption: 51:2; 53:19
resurrection: 1:1; 13-18:10,12;
32-34:2; 36:5; 53:,21; 56:5
revelation: 53:1,5,8
righteous: 29:10
righteousness: 13-18:11; 19:1,2;
22:1; 29:7,10; 30:2; 43:3;
48:1,3,7,9; 50:1; 52:4
sacrifice: 83:1,2
salvation: 67:3; 70:1,2,3; 76:1
sin: 4:1; 6:2;
13-18:3,5,6,8,9,10,11,12; 22:1;
27-28:1,2,3; 29:1,2,6,7,9; 30:3;
31:1,2; 32-34:1,3,4; 35:1,2;
36:2,3,4,5; 37:4,5; 38:1,2; 39:1,3;
40:1,2,4; 42:1; 43:1,3; 44:2,3;
45-46:,2,6,7; 48:1,4,5,6; 50:1;
52:6; 53:16; 70:2; 81:2

slavery: 52:1,2,3,4,6,7,9; 53:3,13
soul: 36:2,3; 42:1; 49:5; 50:2; 51:3; 52:5; 53:4; 54:4; 58:8; 71:4; 72:1,2
spirit: 11:1; 13–18:8,11; 48:7; 50:1; 51:1; 52:1,2,3,4,6,7,8,9; 53:4,16,18,20; 62:17; 71:4
transgression: 29:1,2,4,10; 37:3; 40:4; 45–46:7; 52:6
trespass: 13–18:7; 29:4,6; 30:1,3; 36:2; 40:3; 70:1
vanity: 53:9,10,11; 58:7
will: 13–18:1,12,13; 36:1; 44:1,3; 48:5; 53:1; 54:2; 60:2,15; 61:7; 62:1,3,4,13,14
wrath: 3:1; 9:1,2,3; 23:1; 45–46:7; 63:1
wrongdoing: 6:2

UNFINISHED COMMENTARY

admonish: 18:12; 23:6
angel: 4:8
apostle: 1:3; 2:1,4; 7:1; 15:10; 18:7; 21:4
authority: 3:1; 15:11
baptism: 16:1,3,5,6,8; 18:7,8; 19:2,4,5,6,7,8,11; 21:3; 22:1
baptize: 15:15
begotten: 4:12
blaspheme: 23:6,7
blasphemy: 15:2; 22:3,4,5
bodily: 10:1,4,12; 23:5
body: 5:6,13; 6:2; 10:13; 23:1
call: 2:2; 7:7; 9:3,6
circumcision: 1:3
condemn: 5:14; 9:4; 15:16
confess: 18:11; 23:9
confession: 13:4; 18:14; 23:11,13
correction: 17:4; 22:4
creature: 4:4,8
crime: 14:3; 16:3; 21:6
dead: 10:10; 19:10; 5:1,2,4,6,7,9,10,11,12,13,14,15,16,17; 7:2
death: 5:7; 10:1
deed: 23:5,8
desire: 18:11
despair: 15:10; 22:3
discipline: 1:4; 9:4; 10:3; 18:15
election: 18:14
evil: 8:2; 17:2; 21:2; 23:12
faith: 1:1,4; 3:2; 6:3; 7:3; 8:6; 10:7,13; 15:4; 16:2; 19:2,10; 21:3; 23:2,5
fornication: 16:3
gift: 11:1; 12:7,9; 15:11; 20:5; 23:3
glorify: 10:5
glory: 5:16; 10:7
God: 2:1,3,5; 3:1,2,4; 4:4,6,7,8,10,12; 5:1,3,4,5,6,7,11,12,15,17; 7:1,2,5; 8:1,3,4,6; 9:1,2,3,4,5,6; 10:2,4,5,6,7,8,9,10,11,12; 11:1,2,5,6; 12:2,3,5,7,8,9; 14:1,6,7,8; 15:1,3,4,9,12,13,14; 18:1,3,5,6,7,8,9,14; 19:10,11; 20:3; 21:4; 22:1,2,3,4; 23:1,6,7,9,12,13,14
Gospel: 1:1,2,3; 2:1,5; 3:1,2; 4:5,7; 6:2; 7:1; 10:5,10; 13:3; 18:11; 20:6; 23:15
grace: 1:2,3,4; 6:1,2; 7:3; 8:1,2,4,5; 9:1,6; 10:11; 11:1,2,5; 12:2,3,4,5,8,9; 14:1; 16:2; 18:14; 22:3,4; 23:6,7,12,13,14
heart: 17:2; 19:1; 23:8
hope: 15:11; 17:4; 18:13,14; 21:4
idolatry: 3:5
idols: 4:1
impiety: 3:5; 4:4; 14:1,3; 15:3,16
impious: 5:16; 10:5,6,8; 14:3; 23:13
Jesus: 1:1,2; 2:1,4; 3:3; 4:4; 5:10,15,17; 6:3,4; 7:1,2,4; 8:1,4,6; 11:1,5; 12:2,3,4,5,7,8,9; 14:6,8; 17:1; 23:10,13,14
Jewish: 1:3; 3:2; 6:4; 15:5
Jews: 1:1,4; 3:1; 4:1,3,4; 6:4; 11:3; 14:6; 15:6; 20:2,5; 22:1,4; 23:4,6,12,13
justice: 9:1,6; 10:1,11,12; 23:7

justification: **1**:1
kingdom: **3**:3; **5**:14; **23**:11
law: **1**:1,3,4; **18**:9
life: **2**:3; **5**:2,7,15,16; **6**:2; **13**:4; **22**:1; **23**:12
Lord: **1**:1,2,4; **4**:4,6; **5**:2,6,7,8,9,10,15,17; **6**:3; **7**:2; **8**:1,3,4,6; **10**:12,13; **11**:1,5; **12**:2,3,7,8,9; **13**:3,4,6; **14**:2; **15**:8,9,14; **16**:5; **17**:,4; **18**:4,10,11,15; **19**:2,4; **20**:2,3,4,5; **21**:3; **22**:3,4; **23**:1,6,7,10,11,12,13,14,15
love: **7**:6; **9**:4; **12**:6,7,8; **18**:10,12,14
mercy: **11**:4,5,6; **12**:5,7,8; **15**:16; **16**:4; **21**:5; **22**:2,3; **23**:6
merit: **1**:4; **7**:5,6
nature: **10**:1; **15**:14
obedience: **6**:3; **7**:3
offense: **16**:3
pardon: **10**:9; **15**:,4; **16**:3; **17**:4,5; **18**:5,13,14; **20**:1; **21**:4; **23**:7,12
passion: **19**:2
peace: **8**:1,3,4,5,6; **10**:11,12,13; **11**:1,2,5; **12**:2,3,4,5,7,8,9; **14**:1; **15**:13,16; **18**:12; **22**:2,4; **23**:6,7,12,13,14
pleasure: **13**:7
pride: **1**:4
promise: **15**:4
providence: **13**:2
repent: **9**:2,6; **14**:1; **15**:10; **16**:1; **17**:4
resurrection: **5**:1,2,4,6,7,9,10,11,13,14,15,16,17; **7**:2; **15**:14; **19**:10; **20**:6
righteousness: **9**:4
sacrament: **18**:7,8
sacrifice: **18**:2; **19**:1,2,4,6
salvation: **6**:4; **11**:3; **12**:9; **13**:2,4,6; **15**:8,11; **21**:3
sin: **9**:6; **10**:12; **11**:2; **14**:1,2; **16**:2; **17**:2,3,4,5; **18**:1,2,3,5,14; **19**:8; **20**:1; **21**:3; **22**:3
slave: **2**:1; **7**:1; **21**:7
soul: **18**:11

spirit: **5**:1; **10**:13; **11**:3; **18**:12
synagogue: **2**:1,2,5
trinity: **13**:2,6
unfaithful: **20**:5
will: **18**:1,3,4,5,6,7,8,9,14,15

Index of scriptural citations and allusions (Vulgate)

PROPOSITIONS

Gen.
2:17. **53**:14
Ex.
10:1. **62**:6
Deut.
13:3. **54**:7
21:23. **32−34**:1
29:29. **79**:3
Ps.
2:9. **62**:22
4:3. **53**:11
18:13. **43**:3
59:13. **54**:4
114:3−4. **54**:5
119:3−4. **71**:4
143:4. **53**:9
Prov.
9:17. **39**:2
Eccles.
1:2−3. **53**:10
Sap.
2:12. **6**:3
12:18. **9**:2
13:9. **3**:1
Ecclis.
10:15. **4**:1
Is.
10:22. **65**:2
Hos.
2:24. **65**:2
Mt
5:17. **48**:8
5:44. **71**:1
12:29. **58**:6
15:24. **82**:3
15:26. **82**:3
22:14. **55**:1
22:21. **72**:5
22:37−40. **75**:2
22:42−43. **59**:2
22:43. **59**:3

Lk
2:14. **13−18**:13
Jn
1:1−3. **56**:2
1:29. **32−34**:3
10:16. **65**:3
15:15. **62**:20
Acts
13:46. **82**:2
17:28. **3**:4
Rom.
1:4. **1**:1
1:11. **2**:1
1:18. **3**:1
1:21. **4**:1
1:24. **5**:1
1:28. **6**:1; **62**:10
1:32. **7−8**:1
2:1. **7−8**:2
2:5. **9**:1
2:15. **10**:1
2:26. **68**:3
2:29. **11**:1; **12**:1
3:20. **13−18**:1, 5
3:31. **19**:1
4:2. **20**:1
4:4. **21**:1
4:5. **20**:2
4:15. **13−18**:7; **23**:1
4:17. **24**:1
4:20. **25**:1
5:3. **26**:1
5:5. **60**:6; **61**:7
5:6. **26**:1
5:13. **27−28**:1, 2
5:14. **29**:1, 4
5:16. **29**:5
5:17. **29**:7
5:18−19. **29**:10
5:20. **13−18**:5; **30**:1
6:1. **22**:1; **31**:1
6:6. **32−34**:1

6:12. **13–18**:9
7:2. **36**:1
7:4–6. **36**:2
7:8. **37**:1, 4
7:9. **38**:1
7:10. **38**:2
7:11. **39**:1
7:12. **52**:4
7:13. **37**:4; **40**:1; **43**:1
7:14. **41**:1; **42**:1
7:15f. **43**:1; **44**:1
7:23. **45–46**:1
7:25. **35**:1; **46**:6
8:1. **47**:1
8:3. **32–34**:3; **48**:1
8:7. **49**:1
8:8. **39**:2
8:10f. **13–18**:11; **50**:1
8:11. **36**:5; **51**:1
8:15. **52**:1
8:17–18. **57**:2
8:19–23. **53**:1
8:21. **53**:13
8:23. **53**:17, 19
8:26. **54**:1, 7
8:28. **55**:2
8:29. **55**:3; **56**:1
8:30. **55**:1
8:35. **57**:1
9:5. **59**:1
9:6–7. **69**:2
9:11–13. **60**:1
9:11–15. **61**:1
9:15. **62**:1
9:17. **62**:5
9:18. **62**:11
9:19. **62**:14
9:20–21. **62**:18
9:22. **63**:1
9:24. **64**:1
9:27. **65**:1
9:28. **67**:2
10:1. **66**:1
10:8–10. **67**:1
10:19. **68**:1
11:1. **69**:1

11:11. **70**:1
12:1. **83**:2
12:14. **71**:2
12:17. **71**:2
12:20. **71**:1
13:1. **72**:1
13:3. **73**:1
13:4. **73**:4
13:5. **74**:1
13:8. **75**:1
13:10. **48**:8
13:11. **76**:1
13:14. **77**:1
14:1. **78**:1
14:2. **78**:2
14:3. **78**:3
14:4. **79**:1
14:5–6. **80**:1, 4
14:16. **81**:1
14:22. **81**:1
15:8. **82**:1
15:16. **83**:1
16:17. **84**:1
1 Cor.
  5:1. **79**:1
  5:3–5. **52**:5
  12:6. **60**:12
  13:7. **60**:12
  15:53–54. **51**:2
  15:54. **35**:1
2 Cor.
  5:21. **32–34**:3; **48**:5
  6:2. **76**:1
Gal.
  1:8. **58**:3
  5:24. **32–34**:5
  6:8. **77**:2
Eph.
  2:3. **46**:7
  3:18. **62**:22
  6:6. **74**:3
Phil.
  3:19. **84**:4
Col.
  1:18. **56**:4
  2:15. **58**:4

3:3-4. **53**:6
1 Tim.
  1:3-4. **84**:2
  1:5. **75**:4
  1:20. **52**:5
  2:4. **74**:2
Tit.
  1:10-12. **84**:3
1 Pet.
  2:24. **32-34**:3
1 Jn. 3:2. **53**:7
  3:20. **10**:1

UNFINISHED COMMENTARY

2 Sam.
  11-12. **18**:14-15
  12. **10**:9
Ps.
  109:1. **5**:8
Prov.
  11:31. **10**:5, 8
Is.
  59:1f. **8**:6
Mt
  3:2. **23**:1
  5:44. **18**:10
  7:21. **23**:11
  9:34. **20**:2
  12:22-33. **23**:6
  12:31f. **14**:2
  12:32. **15**:1; **16**:5
  12:33. **22**:4
  15:26. **13**:3
  15:27. **13**:4
  22:15-17. **20**:5
  22:37-40. **18**:9
  22:42-45. **4**:6
  28:11-13. **20**:6
Mk
  2:9-11. **23**:4
Lk
  6:46. **23**:11
  11:5-13. **13**:7
  12:47-48. **18**:4
  17:15-16. **15**:8

Jn
  1:1. **4**:11
  1:3. **4**:11
  1:14. **4**:9
  3:17. **23**:3
  4:7. **15**:8
  4:42. **15**:8
  14:27. **8**:3
  16:33. **10**:12
Acts
  2:1-4. **15**:14
  6:8-7:60. **15**:5
  7:51. **15**:6
  8:9. **15**:9
  8:9-22. **15**:10
  10. **18**:7
  17:28. **3**:4
Rom.
  1:1. **2**:1; **7**:1
  1:2. **3**:2
  1:3f. **4**:2; **5**:1, 6
  1:4. **5**:2; **7**:2
  1:5. **6**:1; **7**:3
  1:6. **6**:4; **7**:4
  1:7. **7**:5; **8**:1; **11**:1
  11:25. **20**:3
1 Cor.
  12:3. **23**:10
  12:10. **20**:4
2 Cor.
  13:4. **5**:7
Gal.
  6:1. **18**:12
Eph.
  2:20. **1**:4
Col.
  1:18. **5**:12
  3:1. **5**:3
2 Thess.
  1:4f. **10**:7
1 Tim.
  1:2. **11**:5
  1:13. **21**:5
2 Tim.
  1:2. **11**:5

Tit.
  1:16. **23**:9
  3:3. **21**:7
Heb.
  6:1f. **19**:10
  10:26. **18**:2; **19**:2
  12:6. **10**:4
Jms.
  1:1. **12**:8
1 Pet.
  1:2–3. **12**:2
  4:6. **10**:10
  4:15–18. **10**:5
2 Pet.
  1:2. **12**:3
1 Jn.
  1:3. **12**:4
  4:9. **7**:6
2 Jn.
  1:3. **12**:5
3 Jn.
  1:1. **12**:6
Jude
  1:1–2. **12**:7

www.ingramcontent.com/pod-product-compliance
Lightning Source LLC
Chambersburg PA
CBHW020807160426
43192CB00006B/468